To Harry Belangy, Joan Berkey, Jim Campbell,
Walt Campbell and Don Pocher

Guardians of History and Good Friends to Boot

400 YEARS of the GHOSTS of CAPE MAY

Chronicling Four Centuries of Hauntings in America's Oldest Seaside Resort

by Craig McManus

featuring the photography of Maciek Nabrdalik

Photography by Maciek Nabrdalik

Story Editors: Kathy DeLuccia & Willy Kare

ISBN-13: 978-0-9785444-3-0

Published by ChannelCraig, Inc.
P.O. Box 651
Ho-Ho-kus, NJ 07423
www.channelcraig.com

TABLET OF CONTENTS

(For the Body of Text)

Backward — 10

Premortem — 12

Native American Spirits — 18

17th Century Haunts — 25

18th Century Haunts — 30

19th Century Haunts — 53

20th Century Haunts — 165

21st Century Haunts — 194

Map of Hauntings — 198

400 Years

of

The Ghosts

of

Cape May

1609-2009

BACKWARD

A PICTURE IS WORTH A THOUSAND WORDS and the purpose of doing a "coffee table" book like this one was to highlight the stunning black and white photography by Maciek Nabrdalik. Maciek has a special way of capturing the *ghostly side* of some of Cape May's most beloved sites. I think it only fitting, on this 400th anniversary of the arrival of English explorer Henry Hudson and his ship the Half Moon (*De Halve Maen*) to give Maciek's work a special position in my ghostly archives.

In this book you will see many new images of America's oldest seaside resort. Along with each grouping of pictures I will give you a little narrative tour of each of these ghostly sites. Not every house is haunted in Cape May, but there are certainly enough buildings with some form of paranormal activity to make one think that for some reason, unknown to the living, Cape May continues to be a stop between Heaven and Earth for the dead.

In addition to returning to some of my favorite haunts in town, I will be exploring other newly unearthed paranormal hot spots. Just when I think I am finished investigating and writing about the ghosts of Cape May, another phone call, letter or email arrives asking me to check out a previously unknown haunt. While many of these queries are excuse the pun, dead ends, quite a few turn out to be legitimate, active haunts. Cape May is indeed the ghostly gift that keeps on giving!

While I will be touching upon some of the more interesting features of each of the haunts pictured on these pages, I will not be going into the great detail I have in *The Ghosts of Cape May Books 1,* 2 and 3. This work has been designed to showcase Maciek's beautiful photographs in a larger format and printed on coated matte paper. His photographic work has been brought to life. Don't worry — most everything else in the book is dead.

Even though the old saying goes, "a picture is worth a thousand words," Maciek's pictures had to compete with me in this book, and I can talk — a lot. I *tried* not to write too much and to let the pictures do the talking, but I just got carried away! The photography and I eventually came to a mutual understanding and I think you will enjoy the finished product as much as I have. For even more detail on some of the newest haunts you will have to wait for my next book, *The Ghosts of Cape May, Book 4.* I shall not keep you waiting too long, don't despair!

Now let's head off on our pictorial journey to the gas lit streets, isolated beaches and dark hallways of some of my favorite haunts in America's oldest — and most haunted — seaside resort. Where the living go to rest and the dead go to live.

OPPOSITE: Cold Spring Cemetery — The final resting place of many of Cape May's dead — at least their bodies anyway.

PREMORTEM

The Days Before the Ghosts

FOR CENTURIES, the peninsula we now call Cape May, New Jersey was nothing more than a vast collection of cedar swamps and marshes protected from the raging waters of the Atlantic Ocean and the calmer surf of the Delaware Bay by numerous shoals (sandbars) and high sandy bluffs.

One can only imagine how peaceful a place the Cape was in those days—not one human soul to break the solemnity of the natural surroundings—the sounds of wildlife, the wind blowing through the tall beach grass and the crash of the surf. The humans—living and dead—had not yet arrived. These were the days before Native Americans and long before the arrival of the first colonists.

My feeling, as a psychic medium and a man who has been working with spiritual energy his entire adult life, is that Cape May has always had a special *charge*. Something makes those who love to come to Cape May keep coming back. I have often referred to the Cape as feeling more like some far off island than a peninsula. Once one crosses the bridge coming into town by the Lobster House, a change in energy is immediately apparent. There is a feeling of well-being that one has just left the busy and chaotic world behind and escaped to a temporary paradise by the sea. This is probably one of the main reasons people have been coming to Cape May so long. It's the feeling of escape.

In the earliest days the Kechemeche Indians summered here, followed years later by the whaling families from New England and Long Island and finally by centuries of seaside loving tourists. We "regulars" all come to Cape May because something draws us here. Almost everyone I talk to about Cape May says the same thing; Cape May makes you feel like you are in a different place and a different time. The energy is as invigorating as the sea air and water itself. The living love it, and so do the dead. Those dead represent hundreds of years of civilization on the Cape.

No one knows for sure when the Native American Indians first arrived at Cape May, but we know they probably came from higher ground by boat, down the Delaware River. In those early days, the peninsula was an isolated wilderness without roads or paths traversing the land.

The Kechemeche Indians were a branch of the Leni-Lenape tribe which itself was an offshoot of the great Algonquin tribe. The Kechemeches came to Cape May in the warmer season to fish, clam, hunt and bathe. They were here long before the first European explorers sailed past Cape May in the fifteenth and sixteenth centuries. Unfortunately, there is very little written record of these early aborigines and most of what we know comes from reports given by some of the earliest European

OPPOSITE: Looking down Higbee Beach toward Sunset Beach

explorers, not from the Native Americans.

The Kechemeches, like other Native American tribes, lived in a culture that was immersed in spirituality and possessed a natural ability to understand the energy of the land and to peacefully coexist with flora, fauna and the Earth itself. They must have been very fond of Cape May. For here these natural hunter-gatherers found an abundance of wild game, fowl and tidal bays filled with clams, oysters and fish. Various historical accounts mention the Kechemeches, but very few accounts go to any length describing the tribe and their culture.

Sir Edmund Plowden, who wrote under the name *Beauchamp Plantagenet*, had been sent by investors and planters in 1648 to investigate the area then known as *New Albion,* between Virginia and Maryland. He notes in his work, *A Description of the Province of New Albion*, the presence of a small tribe of Kechemeches of about fifty men. It is generally assumed that these early Native American visitors came to the Cape in the summer and fall and returned to inner lands in the colder months.

New Jersey's early history is a fascinating topic by itself. However, this book is about ghosts, not the living, and while I will add important historical information when I feel it necessary, I will leave the actual writing of Cape May's early history to others. As Dr. Maurice Beesley and Lewis T. Stevens, two of the first chroniclers of Cape May history, often pointed out, the earliest documented historical information about Cape May is sketchy at best. Much of it was passed down orally from one generation to the next. Many things written as "historical fact" are simply conjecture on the part of a writer. Other important historical facts have been lost to time.

As I try to create some form of written archived history about the ghosts, who they were and how they lived, I often encounter a void in documented evidence about these people and events. It is difficult enough to find personal information for ghosts from the Victorian and Colonial periods, reaching back to the days of the Native Americans and first settlers of the Cape to find accurate historical information is almost impossible. Therefore, I will focus on the ghosts and my experiences with them, and if history illuminates the events, I will add in that information as well.

Some of you may be wondering, if the Kechemeche Indians were here far longer than 400 years ago and if European explorers were sailing past Cape May since the late fifteenth century, why are we only celebrating 400 years of history? Excellent question.

While Cape May and the coastline to the north and south of it were well explored by the early Europeans in the sixteenth century, the general consensus is that very few if any of these ships actually landed at Cape May and explored the land. Further north in New Jersey, even in parts of what is Cape May County today, land was being bought and settled at a quickening pace. However, the lower part of the peninsula was basically cut off from the mainland by huge cedar swamps and marsh. Possessing no inner roadways to civilization, the part of the peninsula we today call the City of Cape May, Cape May Point and Higbee Beach was generally passed over as isolated wilderness by the new colonists. The Kechemeches continued to enjoy their land while the colonists developed and explored other areas.

One of Cape May's most famous visitors in the early times, and the man behind the 400th Anniversary celebration, was barely an overnight guest. Henry Hudson and his ship the Half Moon (*De Halve Maen*) had been searching for a shortcut between the Atlantic and Pacific to the sought after spice islands. The fabled *Northwest Passage* had yet to be discovered, and Hudson and his crew were set upon being the first to find that coveted route. Henry Hudson had actually sailed to America twice before under his native English flag, but failed to produce a route for the English to one up their competitors in the spice trade. The English Crown soon tired of his presence and Hudson went on to solicit the Dutch for work under the auspices of the Dutch East India Company. The Half Moon left with a crew of 20 on March 25, 1609. Robert Juet, one of the ship's crew, documented the trip in his journal.

After hitting ice floes and freezing cold weather conditions near Scandinavia and then near Greenland, Hudson decided to turn the small sailing ship southward, sailing past the Maine coast and all the way south to the Chesapeake Bay. The great bay proved to be another dead end, so Hudson turned the ship north once more and next discovered the Delaware Bay.

Entering the bay on the morning of August 28th 1609, Hudson thought he had finally found the great Northwest Passage to the Pacific Ocean. His enthusiasm was quickly tamed when he hit the first of many sandbars or shoals in the bay. Hudson sailed a short way up the Delaware River until he realized it was full of shoals and too dangerous for a large boat. Heading back down the bay, the Half Moon became stuck close to Cape May on one of those dangerous shoals. The crew decided to spend the night anchored off the peninsula and to wait for the tide to carry them back to sea in the morning.

History gives several accounts of Hudson's visit. None of them can be verified as completely true. One story has the Half Moon crew disembarking, meeting and trading with the Kechemeches, but Juet's log does not mention them leaving the ship for an "overnight stay in Cape May." It only mentions that early the next morning, on August 29th, a storm arrived from the north and blew the ship back out into deeper waters. From this point the crew sailed north and discovered what is now the Hudson River, sailing all the way up to what is today Albany. This was ten years before the Pilgrims landed on Plymouth Rock and Hudson's discoveries had allowed the Dutch to give title to the region. But what about Cape May? Was it of any interest to Henry Hudson and his crew?

It is certainly feasible to think that Hudson would have explored the land on the afternoon of August 28th 1609, since the crew had little choice being grounded. It would not take much effort to launch a small boat with a scouting party on board. Did curiosity get the best of them? What must the crew have thought of this wild and mysterious new land? Would they have been brave enough to risk exploring the dense woods and high dunes of Cape May as the sun was setting into the bay, knowing Native American Indians were probably lurking in the shadows? Could they feel the energy? Were they scared?

It is this very expedition that begins our ghostly history of Cape May. Were there already ghosts on the peninsula when Hudson anchored for the night? Picture yourself, thousands of miles away from home, stuck on a small ship in some unknown bay, tethered to a new and mysterious land. If the ship's crew did not think someone was watching them, they must have been either asleep—or dead.

The Native Americans, who treasured their territory, must have had a sense of forboding upon seeing another foreign ship pulling so close to their summer home. While New Jersey seems to have the honorable distinction of the early settlers actually *paying* the Indian tribes for their land instead of just taking it, the Kechemeches lives and land were now threatened by the arrival of the Europeans. Indeed, their days were numbered and they eventually were crowded out of their summer homes, leaving, with

so many other Indian tribes, for Oklahoma and the western territories. These early inhabitants will always be a part of Cape May history. Their spirit lives on. In fact, quite a few of their spirits still linger — on the shadowy shores of the bay and deep within the woods beyond the dunes. The early history of Cape May and the earliest people are long dead and buried. Luckily, like so many other things that are dead in Cape May, they didn't stay buried very long.

NATIVE AMERICAN SPIRITS

They Went to Their Happy Hunting Ground—It Just Happened to Be Cape May

INTERESTINGLY one of the only truly intriguing bits of information that has been passed down from the time of the Kechemeches was their fascination with the tiny pieces of quartzite we call *Cape May Diamonds*. If you have visited Cape May you have no doubt, at one time or another, picked up a handful of these brilliant little clear stones on the bayside beaches. The Kechemeches felt these stones possessed a special energy, and they collected and traded them. Could Cape May's natural blanket of "diamonds" be creating some sort of energy field? Many healers work with crystals. The idea of using quartz in energy work is not a new one, and Cape May *does* heal the soul!

There are many land masses similar in form to Cape May, but few of these spots seem to radiate such a special energy. I think that Cape May is the east coast's version of Sedona, Arizona. It has a very similar energy, and while Sedona has its ancient rock formations and mountains, Cape May holds its own with its strands of ancient sand speckled with quartz deposits, an aquatic fence of ocean and bay and that marvelous and rejuvenating salt air. Most of all, Cape May has an unseen, but often felt, energy that has been drawing the

living—and the dead to it's shores for over 400 years. There are energy hot spots throughout the world, and Cape May is definitely in the top ten.

I did not go looking for Native American ghosts when I took a team out to Higbee Beach, a long and somewhat isolated section of shoreline on the bayside of the peninsula. I was in fact trying to find old man Higbee's hotel, or what was left of it.

Not having a clue to the whereabouts of the ruins of the hotel (I now know exactly where it is, and I was no where near it at the time) I ventured down Higbee beach from the parking lot near the canal. I could feel the energy was different here. It was much quieter than the ocean side of town, and there were few out on the strand that chilly day.

One of the first landmarks I came upon was the "voodoo tree," a creative bit of wood carving done by some unknown artist to an ancient dead tree at the base of the dunes. The carving had a very haunting presence. Had I known then what I know today about the early Kechemeches, I would have realized that this ancient tree with its contemporary Native American theme was a rather forboding signpost of things to come.

Art is channeled in the same way I channel energy when I contact my Spirit Guides, information comes

OPPOSITE: The Voodoo Tree, since vandalized and cut down, on Higbee Beach

from a higher source. Did the artist who carved this tree sense or channel some of the Native American Spirits in the area?

Deciding to wander off the beach and head over the dunes on one of the many forgotten paths, we made our way into the woods. The sounds of the surf faded and soon even the birds chirping disappeared. Our ghost scouting party had ventured down one of the shadowy, winding trails in search of historical evidence that was more than a half mile away—in the other direction! Luckily in Cape May, if you don't find the ghosts, the ghosts usually will find you.

The energy changed. It was like I had fallen asleep and was now dreaming. The visual landscape was the same, although it began to grow more desolate and isolated the further down the path we traveled. The psychic energy was now different. It was the feeling I experience when I encounter a ghost—like a door opening. I think that was exactly what was happening. A door was opening from some other dimension and two different energies began to merge.

It is in this mix of energies that the living can communicate with, and sense, the dead. The "door" does not usually stay open long, I don't think it is meant to remain open. Something sensed my energy and wanted to move into a place where it could communicate. That something was a group of Native American Spirits.

The name of the tribe that was given to me was "Delaware." This was another name for the Lenni-Lenape tribe. I am not sure if the Kechemeches also called themselves Delawares. Had I encountered a different clan of Indians? The term "sacred land" kept popping into my head. The ghosts were sending me a priority message and were either repeating the words or sending it with enough energy to cause the information to psychically echo.

I began to lose my psychic grounding. I could feel myself becoming uncomfortable with the situation. These ghosts were very strong and obviously had been around longer than any other ghosts I had previously encountered in Cape May. Their energy was starting to wear me down. These were old souls.

I believe we do reincarnate, and ghosts usually connect in personality and name to whomever they were when they last lived. The spirits we encountered were still very connected to their Indian lifetimes and to the land on which we were standing.

At first I thought the Indian ghosts were there to greet us. I soon realized they were there because they still felt the land was their territory, and we were in *their* space. The path had narrowed and disappeared into the natural surroundings. It was time to go back. I gathered the team and realizing there was no sign of any old hotel ruins, we backtracked our way to civilization.

As we hurried back, I could feel the ghosts lunging after us, like a cloud of energy pushing at my back. We moved with haste when suddenly my psychic senses were barraged from another direction. A new ghost, that of a fair-haired young girl *stood in our path*. Why do dead children always have to get in my way when I am trying to hightail it out of a paranormal eruption? Luckily, the Native American ghosts faded, but the little girl did not. She was not part of their energy. She was from another time.

OPPOSITE: An isolated path through the dunes at Higbee Beach.
NEXT PAGE SPREAD: Looking down Higbee Beach toward Sunset Beach

17TH CENTURY HAUNTS

Town Bank—Cape May's Very Own Atlantis

THE LITTLE GIRL belonged to one of Cape May's earliest settlements that went by various names; Town Bank, New England Town, Cape May Town and Portsmouth. She would not give me a name, but she did continue to feed me visual imagery, something ghosts do very well. The image was of a series of small wooden cabins located on a high bluff overlooking the ocean. While I could not be exactly sure, I assumed at the time it was the Town Bank settlement which was located north of where the present canal entrance is, on a stretch of high bluffs that has since washed out to sea. On this side of Cape May one may encounter some of the peninsula's oldest ghostly inhabitants.

While various old historical accounts place settlers from New Haven at the Town Bank site as early as 1640, I think this first group settled further up the shoreline above Cape May county. It appears that the Town Bank group, whalers from Long Island and New England, began their migration to Cape May in the 1670s, possibly earlier.

Historical records show Caleb Carman, one of the first land owners on the Cape, was appointed constable in 1685. Dr. Maurice Beesley points out in his research, that if they needed a constable, there must have existed a town in some form.

The early settlers followed the migrating whales south from New England and the Hamptons. The first Town Bank colony was a small cluster of 15-20 timbered houses erected in close proximity.

In the 1690s, when the West New Jersey Society finally started issuing land titles in the area and the vast plantation of Dr. Daniel Coxe was sold off, more families began migrating from New England and Long Island, New York to set up whaling interests and farms in the new wilderness by the bay. Cape May's genealogy is based on many of these early whaling families, and so are many of the haunts.

As you can see on the map on the next page, the ocean (or bay in this case) was constantly claiming pieces of the early settlement. Today, the Town Bank site sits underwater. As the sea moved in, the people slowly moved back, spread inland and finally settled on the ocean side of the peninsula.

One of the most delightful facts (for this book anyway) is the story about the old graveyard at Town Bank. In those days the idea of exhuming bodies and moving burial places was not as appealing as moving houses. Over the years I had heard stories about the headstones of the early settlers being moved to Cold Spring Cemetery, but the bodies were left behind and slowly were being washed into the surf. Fabulous.

OPPOSITE: What's left of the Town Bank Colony is now a little damp.

Posing that question to my good friend and Cape May historian Jim Campbell, it seems that only one gravestone was moved to Cold Spring and the rest were left behind. When the canal was dredged for ferry service in the 1960s, the dredges began to pull up pieces of headstones. Some of those gravestones, I am told, were used as decorative stones in fireplaces in Cape May. (And one wonders why we have so many ghosts!)

A Leaming family member reports in an early Cape May diary of people seeing the graves slowly washing into the bay and noting that the graveyard and houses had eventually all but vanished. Coffins and bodies washing into the surf as the sun sets over the bay. Delightful.

When I was young, my Aunt Ella and Uncle Bob had a home inland in the Town Bank section of Cape May where the government had erected HUD housing in the 1960s. Little did I realize I was so close to the original Cape May housing development!

Being nearer to the bayside, my uncle would drive us to the beach next to the canal. One of my favorite things to do was to walk out to the end of the long rock jetty (pictured next page.) There was something energizing about the area. One of my fondest memories of Cape May in the late 1960s is sitting on the bayside beach and the jetty, watching the sun set over the water. It was only recently, when I read an email from Jim Campbell about the canal dredging, that it all clicked into place. Those engineers were dredging in the area around where the jetty now rests. Since Town Bank would be hundreds of feet out in the water now, the jetty would basically be a bridge to that spot.

All those years, before I knew I was psychic, I would sit on the end of that jetty for hours without realizing I was probably sitting right on top of Cape May's original settlers! That jetty is literally a walkway to the dead. Try it sometime, it's fun.

Technically, if the canal followed the New England Creek and if we take the old map as historically accurate, the settlement was a little further north of the canal entrance, but no one really knows for sure. The map shown right that was supposedly copied from an early 1726 map of Portsmouth or Town Bank, by Russ Lyons in 1951, for the Cape May Geographical Society. According to historian and author Joan Berkey, no trace of the original 1726 map exists today. On the map one can see the receding shoreline from 1605 to 1868. Like elsewhere on the peninsula, the high bluffs of Town Bank slowly dissolved into the sea.

If someone died at Town Bank and stayed behind as a ghost, what would they see today? Their former home is now underwater and no longer on a high bluff. My theory is some see the landscape change. These ghosts will adapt. Others refuse to admit they are dead and will cling to their final resting place or haunt where they had lived. While I have encountered ghosts on the bayside, like the little girl, I cannot say for sure if they are from the first settlement. That was a long time ago and ghosts do eventually move on.

I can vividly recall one summer boat ride with friends on the bay. We had decided to anchor so a few of the boating party could take a dip. I remember sitting in the boat and waiting for my friends to finish. The water was deep and I decided to sit out the swim. As I waited, I felt an eerie pull from below. I was being watched — from down under.

Had we unknowingly anchored on top of the old graveyard? I started to visualize people reaching up from the bottom, as if they were trying to grab at our feet. I thought this was surely my overactive imagination when suddenly one of my friends exclaimed something had just cut his foot! Old junk? Imagination? Ghosts? Hmmm...

OPPOSITE: A rendering based on an old map of the Town Bank settlement as it appeared in 1726. (Courtesy of The Greater Cape May Historical Society)

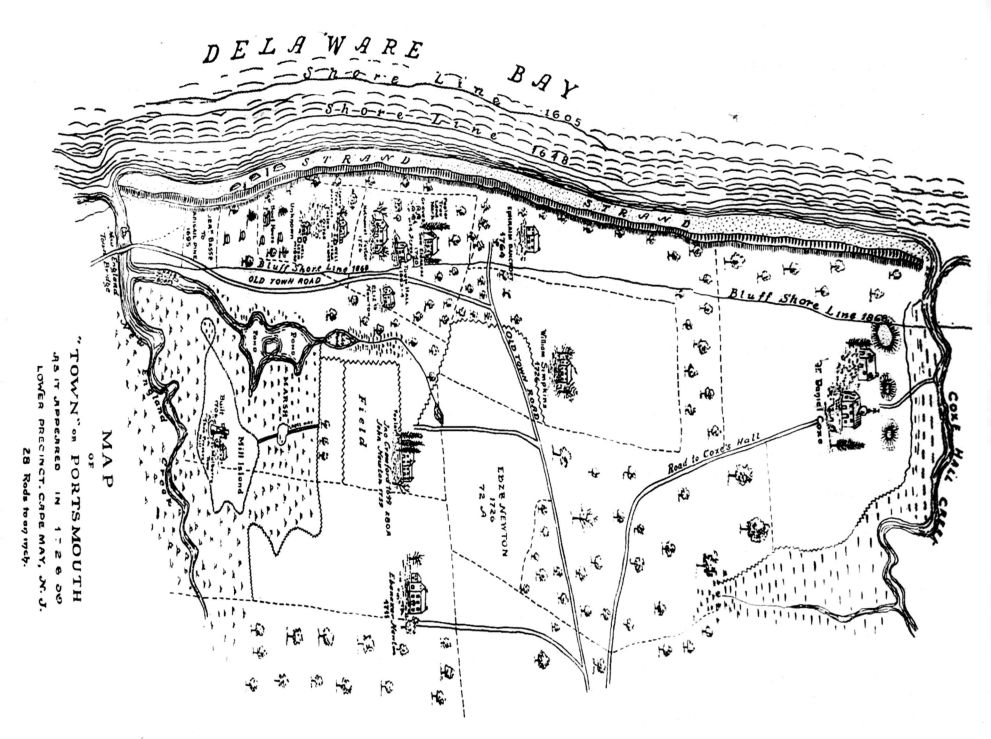

Map of Town Bank or Portsmouth as it appeared in 1726

27

28

18TH CENTURY HAUNTS

Whalers Turned Farmers Turned Ghosts

A S THE SEA continued to swallow up the high bluff and low beaches on the bayside of Cape May, including the small Town Bank settlement, the early pioneers, at least the ones who were not buried there, began to move inland.

By the early 1700s, all that was left of the old whaling colony was a collection of farms dotted with ruins of the original settlers' homes. A few of the tombstones from the early graveyard were moved to Cold Spring. The rest, along with the bodies beneath them, slowly washed into the bay and are now, along with that early settlement, deep beneath the surf. You've heard of the old expression, "Someone's walking over your grave?" In Cape May we say "Someone's swimming over your grave."

Most of the Cape May peninsula and a large portion of southern New Jersey originally belonged, in the late 1600s, to Dr. Daniel Coxe, an esteemed English physician whose patients included Charles II and Queen Anne. Coxe held the title to many pieces of land including a huge tract in Cape May.

While he never actually came to America, Coxe did keep a large plantation on the bay side above Town Bank where he erected Coxe Hall, a meeting place for all of the residents of the settlement. After Coxe began to liquidate his American holdings in the 1690s, land titles began to pass to the first settlers. This is really where the true early history, and hauntings of Cape May, begin. The people had arrived, their ghosts would soon follow.

Cape May County is rich in early history and (luckily for me) rich in early ghosts. While some ghosts seem to remain in their dwellings for centuries, most eventually do cross over.

We are creatures of habit and we habitually get bored with things. Ghosts, human souls without the body, also get bored doing the same thing year after year. After a few centuries those souls probably make the leap to the Other Side out of shear boredom. How long could *you* stay in your room?

One of the highlights of ghost hunting is all of the great living people that one comes to know. While writing this book, I had the pleasure of (finally) meeting historian and writer Joan Berkey. Joan's book, *Early Architecture of Cape May County*, is packed with historical facts and pictures of Cape May's earliest houses and settlements, some of them places that I have written about in my books. If you love early history and are a Cape May fan, this book is a must read.

The Memucan Hughes House

P ROBABLY THE FIRST really old house that caught my psychic attention in Cape May was the Memucan Hughes or "Colonial House" set back behind Alexander's Restaurant and next to the Police Department on Washington Street. The exact age of this old dwelling/tavern was a matter of debate for many years. First it was thought to be 1760s, the most recent thinking was it was built around 1800, making the house not Colonial at all.

Historian Joan Berkey very recently found evidence to the contrary, however, that the structure may date back to 1730, making this house one of the oldest standing structures in Cape May City. The older the structure, the more chance of it being haunted. Layers of history converging on one spot have a

OPPOSITE: The Memucan Hughes House—one of Cape May's First Taverns

ABOVE: Sometimes in a ghost investigation the writing is on the wall.
In the case of the Colonial House, the writing is on the window,
etched in glass 200 years ago by one of the early living occupants
of the house, Elizabeth Eldredge. Could Elizabeth now be one of he
ghostly family that hides in the attic of the old house?

way of bringing out the best in ghosts and the best ghosts.

The Colonial House is now a museum run by the Greater Cape May Historical Society. If you want to visit a real haunted house, but do not want to spend the night, this is the place to go. While the downstairs museum area is somewhat active, the real hot spot is the third floor attic area. Once you get past the old timber door with its many locks, and ascend the winding staircase, you will find the paranormal heart of the Memucan Hughes House. Beyond that old door the undead linger.

Who exactly is haunting here is a matter of question. Many tour-goers report seeing a figure in the third floor window, but cannot tell if it is a man or a woman. This house has also yielded a bounty of EVPs (Electronic Voice Phenomena) for myself and other investigators. Both male and female voices have been captured on tape.

One of the ghosts I sensed in the house gave me the name "Sarah." As far as I have been able to check, there has not been a Sarah associated with the house. However, ghosts *are* transient and, as this building was one of Cape May's first taverns, there may have been a "Sarah" who worked there.

This house is thought to have originally been built by the Eldredge family of West Cape May, and was most likely moved here from a spot on Jackson Street where Cape Savings stands today. Since the house has had so many owners and is one of the last remaining early period houses in town, it is quite possible that the ghosts are early as well. Whatever is lurking in the Colonial House is locked behind that old attic door. Someone at one point in history put multiple locks on that old door and I would suggest keeping those locks in good working order! You can read the entire story in *The Ghosts of Cape May Book 2*.

33

Coxe Hall Cottage

ONE OF THE MOST unique collections of old houses in Cape May is, literally, a collection. Historic Cold Spring Village was begun in 1973 when Dr. Joseph Salvatore and his wife Patricia Anne rescued the old Grange Hall at Cold Spring and moved it to a 22-acre site nearby. I will be delving more deeply into these old houses in *The Ghosts of Cape May Book 4*, due out in 2010. In the meantime, I want to tell you about a few of the more active haunts in the "village" that you can visit, like Coxe Hall Cottage.

There is not much to see in the old cottage, but there is quite a bit to feel. A woman's ghost is *very* attached to that house and she seems to be in contact with the ghost of a man nearby.

This building has moved around quite a bit. It stood for many years attached to another dwelling on Jonathan Hoffman Road before being moved to the Village and restored by the Salvatores. Current thinking is that this cottage was originally part of a much larger building called Coxe Hall. Dr. Daniel Coxe, who owned thousands of acres of land in Cape May, had a great hall built in 1691 at Town Bank to be used for meetings and religious services. Although Dr. Coxe never set foot on American soil, the hall was well used by many of the earliest settlers.

This woman seems to have been a servant of some kind and holds up long strands of yarn, as if checking the length. When she realized I was psychically watching her, she vanished toward the

LEFT: Circa 1691 Coxe Hall Cottage—What's left of Dr. Daniel Coxe's Hall (besides the ghosts) Originally built at Town Bank. RIGHT: Craig searching for ghosts at Historic Cold Spring Village.

stairs. Sometimes ghosts want company, sometimes they want to be left alone.

When I step inside a structure like Coxe Hall Cottage, my mind becomes inundated by historical and psychic residual energies. When I channel people's loved ones from the Other Side, they want to communicate with me. If I try to talk to ghosts, they typically have difficulty communicating or will not communicate with me at all.

What makes this particular old structure a real psychic challenge is that it, along with its ghosts, has literally been around the block many times. This house has seen many occupants over the last 318 years. Even my friend and Cape May historian Walt Campbell's grandfather lived in this house. A long history coupled with an elusive ghost makes my work really difficult.

The thing that intrigues me about Cold Spring Village is that many of the ghosts came with the structures and quite a few have since moved in. When I first visited here I could sense a few dead types lurking around, but as I continued to revisit these dwellings I soon realized I had, excuse the pun, unearthed an entire ghost community!

When a house is occupied by a living family, ghosts tend to move out of the way. When a house is unoccupied for long periods of time, ghosts tend to move in for a while. If those same ghosts happen to find houses like those in Cold Spring Village, fully furnished with all the latest in historical trappings, the ghosts will not just come for an extended visit, they will make themselves right at home—permanently.

PICTURED: Inside one of the haunted houses at Cold Spring Village

The Whilldin-Miller House

ONE OF MY FAVORITE OLD HAUNTS in Cape May, actually West Cape May, the Whilldin-Miller House has seen many famous names in Cape May history come and go. Luckily a few have decided not to leave just yet. According to Joan Berkey, who researched this structure down to the nails and studs, the rear section of the house was either built circa 1695 by Joseph Whilldin Sr. (1665-1728) or built by his son Joseph Whilldin Jr. (1693-1748) around 1715.

The house was run as a tavern in the 1760s, and possibly also an inn, by Joseph Jr.'s son, James Whilldin, Esq. (1714-1780.) Local lore also has the house being used as a hospital during the American Revolution.

While the front section (right) which was built by Jonas Miller in 1860 for one of his daughters, shares in the paranormal activity, the rear section (shown left) seems to be most active.

In 1981 the house was converted to a restaurant. Each time I have dined there *something* strange has occurred. A lamp has tossed itself off of a sideboard, silverware has moved by itself and even a total blackout occurred for about thirty seconds one evening after I asked the ghosts to "give me a sign" that they were present by flickering the lights. The waiters came rushing out to my table exclaiming, "Mr. McManus! You did it again!" implying that my presence had set the ghosts buzzing. It was after I found out that the lights had gone out all the way up to Wildwood that I started to question the power of my own transmitter! Of course, it was only a coincidence—wasn't it? One of the ghost's names here is Catherine, who may have been a servant of Jonas Miller's family. There is also a male spirit in uniform that some have witnessed walking the grounds. Go here for the food—and the ghosts.

OPPOSITE: The Whilldin-Miller House in West Cape May, currently incarnated as the Moonfish Grill.
ABOVE: The house as it appeared in the 1930s when it was called the Fow House. (Courtesy of Walt Campbell)

The David Cresse House

THIS OLD HOMESTEAD in Lower Township is a great haunt because it has been in the same family since it was built around 1828. Like other historic haunts in Cape May, this house also has a much older section attached at the rear. According to historian Joan Berkey the rear kitchen section of the house was moved here from an unknown location and was built between 1700-1730. The main section of the house was built around 1828 by David Cresse (1799-1849) on land that his wife Maria Leaming (1806-1875) inherited from her father, Spicer Leaming (1762-1838.)

David Cresse may be long dead and buried, but his wife Maria is still alive (I mean dead) and kicking. She roams this old house watching over everything and everyone—living and dead. I spent one warm summer evening with Martha Kesler and her mother Martha exploring the old house. You can read the entire story in *The Ghosts of Cape May Book 2.*

This house has several generations of ghosts, including Maria Leaming Cresse who still occupies the same bedroom she slept in almost 200 years ago. Maria is definitely the matriarch of this ghostly group. Throughout my entire visit she was with me both physically and psychically. One of the most unusual things I saw here were phantom handprints that have appeared through the paint on the living room ceiling. While one could write this off as the work of some careless painter, that does not explain the phantom *footprints*—also on the ceiling! They are small, like those of a child and knowing Cape May—probably a dead child.

Lower Township contains many of Cape May's earliest houses, with many early inhabitants keeping these same houses occupied. The David Cresse house is haunted by ghosts who are all related. One theory I have about hauntings is that one family member haunting tends to draw in other family members into the paranormal mix. Picture when your time finally comes. You start to cross over when and you happen to notice your grandparents or parents sitting around your old house. Wouldn't you turn around and go back to greet them? Maybe this is how it works. Some of us want to cross because we have no one left here. Others do not want to leave their living family and friends. What if those family members and friends were dead, but still here—would you join them in the parlor for a game of cards?

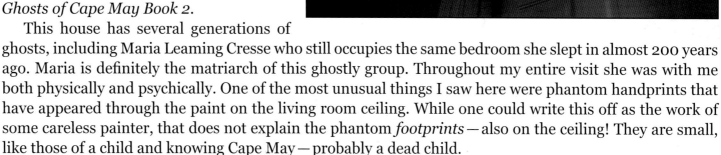

OPPOSITE: The Circa 1828 David Cresse House. ABOVE: The mysterious hand and footprints on the ceiling of the parlor. 41

The Joshua Hildreth House

THIS VENERABLE old Rio Grande home, built sometime in the 1720s or 1730s by either David Hildreth or his son Joshua, is the site of multiple hauntings. The house is now the site of Winterwood, a Christmas and holiday shop that also has a (haunted) location in Cape May City. The sign outside the shop will tell you the house is haunted by Hester Hildreth. However, Hester has gone a haunting elsewhere. I have encountered her rambling ghost several times in Cape May City, but never in Rio Grande. It seem she left her familial homestead in search of more spacious quarters, as the Christmas shop had crowded her out.

This lovely old property comes complete with its own family burial ground, where the last remains of several Hildreth and related family members rest. The remains are at rest, the souls are quite the opposite. Two of the children buried in that plot are behind all of the moving toys, missing keys, phantom voices, frantic footsteps and other playful acts that are characteristic of something a (dead) child or children would be doing. These two children have been active for many years and I am certainly not the first ghost hunter to come here. In fact, several well-known parapsychologists came down from New York to investigate this house back in the 1970s. Ghosts of children act like children. They may now be hundreds of years old, but they still think like they are young. This house is psychically buzzing. There may even be more ghosts here, but I have not returned to unearth them at this time. Cape May City keeps me busy enough!

A house full of Christmas decorations and toys of all sorts. What better place for kids to hang out? It is sad to think of children being forgotten by their families to become orphan ghosts. Is this type of situation more common in the afterlife? Years later, these children probably have little memory of their parents and now exist with each other as their only source of companionship.

Hester's body rests in the Rio Grande Cemetery. Her ghost is too busy haunting Cape May to stop and sleep. Now that malls have replaced the quiet fields that used to surround the old burial ground, there is surely no rest for the dead. And people wonder why Cape May is so haunted.

OPPOSITE: The Joshua Hildreth House, now incarnated as Winterwood.

The John Hand House

MOST OF THE TIPS I receive about new haunts come from the owners or occupants of the buildings in question. Sometimes I happen to find a new haunt by association. Someone I am investigating mentions a friend or neighbor who has had ghost experience. One of these "haunts by association" was the John Hand House located on Washington Street near the Emlen Physick Estate.

I had been ghost hunting with Linda Hadrava and her family at their Victorian home next to the Physick Estate when one of the ghosts who identified herself as "Alice" mentioned I should visit the old house across the street. She also kept repeating the name "Hand." Linda Hadrava told me there was an old Hand House diagonally across from them and remembered hearing that a man in a tricornered hat had been seen by renters, walking through the living room.

Taking Alice up on the offer, we got permission from her neighbor, Harry Dean, to check out the house. The first thing that struck me was the plaque on the outside wall stating the house had been built by John Hand in 1712. When you are used to being surrounded by Victorian architecture and ghosts, the thought of an ancient house sitting in the middle of all that gingerbread harboring a few Colonial ghosts is intriguing to say the least. At the time this early period house was built Washington Street wasn't even on the map. John Hand had purchased 300 acres here, apparently from the English. The house has been remodeled over the centuries and driving by, one would hardly recognize it as Colonial. Once inside however, that all changes. It's a psychic throw back in time.

John Hand and his wife Mercy Crowell Hand are still at home on their old plantation. I often wonder exactly what they see. When we lose these vessels we call bodies and our soul is free to float around, what do we perceive? Do we see energy imprints of physical matter? Do things appear as they were when we lived—or does the scenery change with the times?

I run a tape along with each investigation to document what I am feeling and sensing on a psychic level. I am usually describing the energies to the owners or occupants of the dwelling and answering questions at the same time. Replaying the tape helps me to write a report after the investigation. It may also capture a few EVPs or ghostly voices, an added bonus for any ghost hunter.

Someone or something did not want us recording them the evening I went back to the John Hand House to meet with Harry Dean, his wife and the Hadravas. My portable recording deck froze and locked down on the tape and has never worked since. We then tried to use one of Harry's tape recorders and that too malfunctioned! Finally, Linda Hadrava's husband Dan brought over a boom box he had and *finally* we were able to record.

The ghost of Mercy Hand was benevolent and low key. She answered several questions before fading into the ethers. As I channeled further, I announced to the group "John Hand is here." The room got ice cold and strange bluish lights moved along the wall behind me. Everyone saw and felt a change in the room. Each ghost has a feeling and energy all its own. John Hand was intense. Read more about him and his house in *The Ghosts of Cape May Book 2*.

　　　OPPOSITE: The Circa 1712 John Hand House

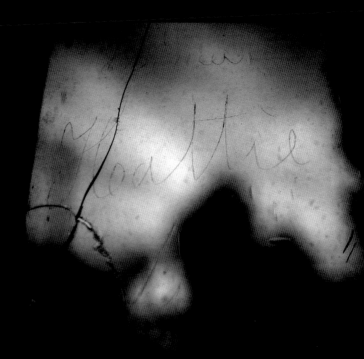

A T ONE TIME, the Borough of West Cape May was called Eldredge. The small community was named for the old Cape May family that had settled the area in the eighteenth and nineteenth centuries. Today quite of few of the original settlers are still in town. It seems people who live in Cape May never quite get the cue to move on!

Because Cape May suffered from several devastating fires in the late 1800s, much of what is today the downtown area was rebuilt after 1878. The oldest houses were mostly destroyed by the Great Fire of 1878. A few did survive outside of the fire's reach, but if you want truly early homes, you need to look outside of the city in areas like West Cape May and Lower Township. Here you will find a treasure trove of historical dwellings–and historical ghosts to match.

The Thomas Eldredge, Jr. House on Broadway in West Cape May is a lovely inn that has a few extra unseen guests. I have sensed three ghosts here: a young child, a ghost who calls himself George who may be a previous owner of the house from the 20th century, and Henry S. Eldredge, Thomas Eldredge Jr.s' son who drowned two days before his 25 birthday on March 12, 1888, while working on a pilot boat .

This house is actually two houses put together. The left side of the house (as you look at the picture opposite) is thought to date from around 1780-1820. The right side dates to the 1840s. Both sections are thought to have been moved here and assembled into one home. When you move someone's house, whether he or she is dead or alive, that person or persons will usually follow along for the ride.

My first ghost encounter here was with the child who lead me to the window with the name "Hattie" etched in it. I thought her name was Hattie, but it turned out the Hattie who carved the name, Harriet Sawyer Eldredge Stevens, died at age 43 in 1904. Was the ghostly girl trying to tell me something, or was she just pointing out something unique about the house?

This house demonstrates how a haunted dwelling can host ghosts of different time periods, in the same space, who interact with each other as if time means nothing.

Maybe the ghosts know something we don't.

ABOVE: Harriet "Hattie" Eldredge has left her signature in perpetuity etched in glass in her old bedroom.

Cold Spring Church Cemetery

CEMETERIES are the last place you will find a ghost. Ghosts haunt where they lived, rarely where they are buried. However, because Cape May is extra special in the paranormal department, our local historic cemetery at the Cold Spring Church is allowed to have a few ghosts of its own.

Seriously, the place is spooked. I have spent quite a bit of time crisscrossing the old graveyard in search of this dead person or that dead person for historical information. While I am actually looking for a physical body or rather a physical gravestone over a body, something always manages to start clinging to my energy.

This cemetery goes back to the 1700s and has seen most of Cape May's well known citizens drop in for a visit. Why some of these ghosts hang out at a cemetery is beyond me. Come on folks, you're at the beach. Get some sun, hit the waves!

One theory about ghosts who haunt cemeteries is that they are so attached to their physical lives, they cannot let go of their physical bodies. Some ghosts seem to sit and stare at their own gravestones in disbelief, others stay near the gravestones of a loved one. Eventually these ghosts move on and cross over to Heaven. For some, the realization that life is over takes hundreds of years.

At Cold Spring Cemetery (pictured in the previous spread and opposite) I have encountered many ghosts of children. While childrens' ghosts are very prevalent in Cape May, one would not expect a group of children to be hanging out in a cemetery. Yet they do.

When a child dies and does not cross over to Heaven, he usually tries to stay with the family as a ghost. If the child died when the family was not present, that ghost may wander in search of his or her family and become lost along the way. The ghostly children of the Cold Spring churchyard seem to have adopted one another. Are they somehow tethered to the spot where their bodies rest, or do they come here to play, as living children might?

Next time you feel like digging up a little history, take a ride over to the Cold Spring Church and stroll through the churchyard. Just make sure to ask whatever ghost happens to get into your car to leave before you start the ignition.

19TH CENTURY HAUNTS

The Golden Age of Ghosts

IN 1869 and 1878, two great fires swept through the heart of the city of Cape May and changed the landscape and architecture from Colonial to Victorian with a one-two punch. While the 1869 fire was more localized to the business district, the great 1878 fire wiped out more than 30 acres of the resort community. It was decided to rebuild in a contemporary style. The old Colonial days were out, the high Victorian days were in, and that change defines Cape May to this day.

The haunts I have covered thus far have been spread out around Cape May's perimeter and further out in West Cape May and Lower Township. Luckily, the fire spared those sections of the peninsula and left us with at least a partial snapshot of Cape May's early days.

As far back as the 1760s there were advertisements in Philadelphia newspapers enticing people to the cool beaches of Cape May. While fishing and farming kept many residents busy, the tavern and inn owners knew they had a good thing going at Cape May, word just needed to get out to the inner cities. By the early 19th century, ships carrying passengers from Baltimore, Philadelphia and other ports were landing in Cape May, America's cool new seaside resort.

With the increase in customers, Cape May also began to see an increase in deaths and, luckily for me, ghosts as well. Here are some of my favorite 19th Century haunts in Cape May. This is by no means a complete list—that would take volumes!

One of the most recent investigations I have been working on is the house of Cape May's very own coffin maker, Isaac Smith, Jr. (pictured left) Now owned by the Craig family, this venerable old home has some long term ghostly guests.

When I recently visited with Rona Craig and her daughter Betsy, I told them they had a lady ghost by the name of "Ruth." Ruth began telling me details about the house that I could not have known as I had never set foot inside the dwelling to date.

One of the things that usually surprises people who have a ghost is just how cognizant some ghosts can be. As I mentioned a few pages back, we really do not know how a ghost perceives their world or ours. What I can tell you from experience is that some ghosts are *very* aware of their surroundings and seem to watch over everything. This was Ruth.

The first thing Ruth complained to Rona about was that the front door had not yet been fixed. Neither Rona nor Betsy had mentioned anything to me about the door, and in fact it had been in need of repair for at least two weeks prior. She mentioned it kept sticking—referring to the old lock.

OPPOSITE: The Circa 1820 Isaac Smith, Jr. House

Someone asked Ruth where she stayed in the house. "The attic," was the answer, "Near the little door by the cracked glass on a wall. Then she talked about "notches" in the rafters used to measure someone long dead. The Craig's lead me up the winding stairs to the old attic, revealing to me not one, but two small doors. By the door, leading to an outside deck was a small mirror stuck to the wall, with a *crack running through it!*

The Craigs were amazed at how sentient their ghost was and how much she watched over the house. While I have yet to find a Ruth associated with the house, there is no doubt whoever she is, she is right at home.

Ghosts are very often misunderstood. We have been brainwashed by Hollywood that all ghosts are out to get us. Ghosts are simply souls without a body. People we cannot see. They are in death who they were in life.

I recently spoke with Betsy Craig about the house. She told me she had been speaking with a lady named Liz who grew up in the house. Liz confirmed the presence of notches in the attic. She knew exactly where they were — as did the ghost. Like many haunts found in Cape May, someone is *always* home. At the old coffin maker's house, her name is *Ruth*.

Now one could say anyone could have taken a wild guess about a door sticking in an old house like this and probably been right most of the time, but there was more — much more.

ABOVE: The sticking door and lock at the Isaac Smith Jr. House - OPPOSITE: The old, dark attic above.

The William Eldredge House
(Highland House Inn)

IF A HOUSE COULD TALK, this would be that house. The William Eldredge House is thought to have been built as far back as 1820. It has years and years of history between its walls and with ghosts, walls *can* talk.

One of the great things about this Inn is it's location in West Cape May outside of the busy Cape May City limits *and* it is pet friendly. An added bonus is that the old house is also haunted and these ghosts can talk!

While I was investigating Highland House, as it is now called, I was running a cassette tape recorder to take notes and to try to capture a few EVPs. Typically, the EVPs will be snippets of conversations or words that will seldom make sense in context to the questions one will ask. For instance, if I asked the ghosts, "What are your names, please?" the response might be "I'm in the garage." It's like the ghost has ADD instead of me! This is not to say all EVPs are word salad. I have had ghosts answer questions on tape, though it is rare to get a good give and take interview with a ghost. At Highland House, you ask a question, you get an answer. These ghosts are so in tune with our Earthly energy, they hear and respond to questions. Highland House gives good EVP.

Apparently Enoch Eldredge, William's brother, is also haunting this house along with a few other dead Eldredges. This entire section of West Cape May was one big Eldredge tract in the 1800s, and it seems like the family still goes a callin'!

Ghosts are transient beings. They move around and interact. Don't be disappointed if you do not encounter a ghost here. The Eldredges are very busy being dead.

The Ewing-Douglass House

IT IS USUALLY on a warm summer day that I find myself wandering around Historic Cold Spring Village and being a sugar-holic, I will eventually make my way to the ice cream parlor, housed in the old Ewing-Douglass House. This house has almost as many ghosts as it does ice cream flavors.

Thought to have been built by farmer David Ewing on his property on Town Bank Road in Lower Township around 1850, the house was eventually sold in 1869 to another area farmer, Nathaniel Douglass, who used part of the house as his country store.

I am always surprised at the response I get when I ask people who work in an old house if they have any ghost experience. The usual response is for them to look around, check that no one is listening and then give me their ghostly confession.

I had sensed a woman in the upstairs window of the house several times. I finally inquired to the lady working in the ice cream parlor just who that woman might be. The manager of the shop immediately could relate to my story as others had reported also seeing a woman in the upper window! I was then offered a self-guided tour of the upper floors of the house. I asked the ladies (the living ladies) present at the ice cream parlor not to give me any other details about their experiences until after I finished.

Here is a house with two completely different sets of energy. On the second floor I encountered the ghost of a vivacious younger boy, maybe nine or ten years old. He could see me and hear me and was totally aware the house was fully equipped with the latest in ice cream flavors and accessories. His energy felt disconnected from the house, like he was visiting instead of living there. As I tried to make a stronger connection with him, he vanished through a wall. The strange thing about this exit is that he would have literally walked into thin air as there was no room on the other side of that particular wall. Was there an earlier structure that is not now extant? Ghosts usually follow a preexisting pattern of travel inside a dwelling. He was gone and out of my psychic sight completely.

I then noticed another old door and opened it, revealing a winding staircase to the attic. As I slowly trudged up the creaking old steps (all I needed was an oil lamp and a thunderstorm to complete the mood) I could sense a different energy. The mood changed, and in my mind I could see a woman sitting by the window sewing. She was gazing out into the Village and did not notice me at all.

I did not "see" this woman with my eyes. I "saw" her with my mind. She was in her thirties, I think. She looked perfectly fine, and I was not picking up anything about her that was distressing. The problem was I was not picking up *anything* about her at all. It was all visual and nothing communicative. Like watching a TV show with the volume turned off. She continued to sew and gaze out the window and that was it. This may have been what is called a *residual haunting*. This is a form of energy trapped in the ethers of a place that continues to broadcast the same visual loop, over and over again.

This is a paranormally interesting house. More about this in *Book 4*. Until then you can visit the haunted ice cream parlor yourself, but mind the cold spots—they could be more than just dessert!

OPPOSITE: The Ewing-Douglass House, circa 1850, now the ice cream parlor at Historic Cold Spring Village.

CAPE MAY was a lot smaller in 1850. The landscape would continue to change as the years went on with expansion of the city and then two devastating fires in 1869 and 1878. We are not quite sure what the ghosts see. Do they see the way things were when they lived or do they see how things have become since they died?

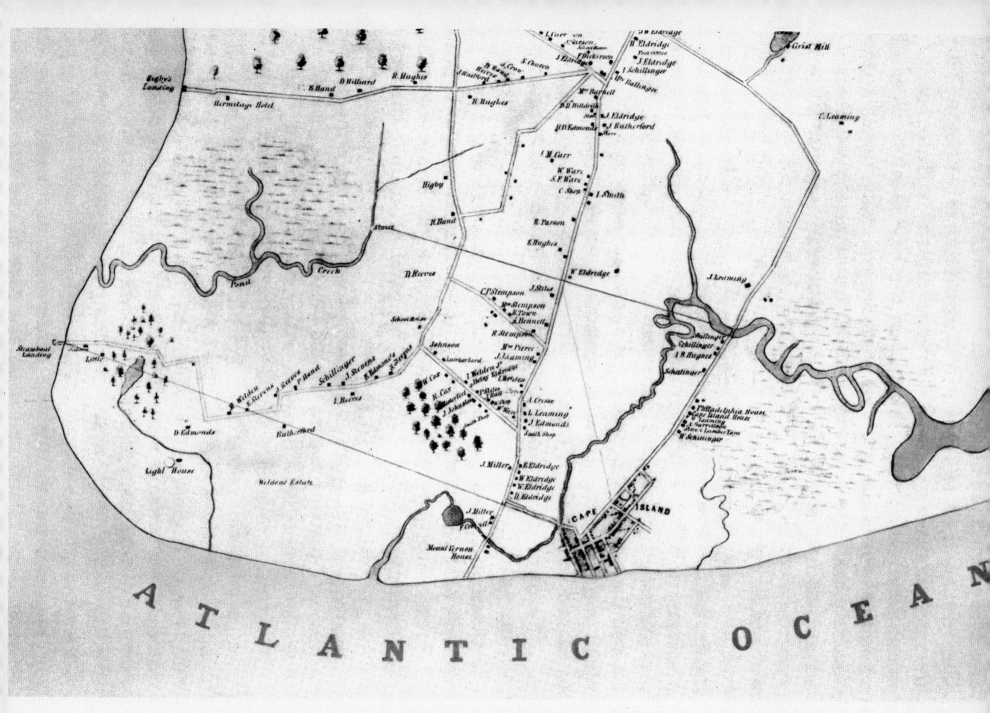

Map of Cape May—1850

ALONG WITH Ludlam House, the old Reeves homestead is one of my top five favorite haunts in Cape May and one of my favorite ghost stories.

Captain John W. Reeves fought in the Civil War in the battle of Williamsburg. He fought alongside John McCrea and reported McCrea's death and burial in a letter to his wife Hannah.

John Reeves built his home on what is today called Stevens Street after buying the property in 1867. Another structure, a toll house, was built on the corner of this same property and faced Sunset Boulevard. If the two structures were eventually combined to form one structure, that information is not known at this time. There is a lot we do not yet know about this haunt, but I'm working on it. These things take time.

We do know that Captain Reeves still resides in the old house in West Cape May, and that several of his Reeves relatives are haunting right along with him. Jenny Reeves, John's young cousin who died around the age of seven, is very attached to current owner Beth Bozzelli's family and seems to know everything about them. When I first channeled her spirit in a third floor room that she frequents in the house, Jenny knew all of the old toys Beth's children used to play with and where they were now stored in the attic. She knew about a pair of "purple shoes in a trunk" that Beth's daughter confirmed as having kept from her childhood. They were packed away in the very trunk in the attic Jenny was referring to! Some ghosts become just like family members, whether or not the living members of the family know it. Jenny was very "talkative" and wanted to let Beth and her family know she loved them and the house. Beth and her family have learned to peacefully coexist with their ghosts.

Captain John Reeves on the other hand did not communicate with me directly, other than to allow me to sense his presence. He came and went very quickly. He also has the uncanny ability of being able to show up in mirrors, something that Beth Bozzelli has experienced firsthand. Why some ghosts are seen and some only show their reflections probably has more to do with the observer than the ghost. A mirror can be a focal point for the mind's attention, like the old divination method of *scrying*, where one focuses on a crystal ball, mirror or other reflective surface and receives images in the mind of places, people and events. This could be why some ghosts, like Captain Reeves, are only seen in mirrors or windows. Did I mention the secret trap door under the stairs?

You can read the whole story in *The Ghosts of Cape May Book 3*. It is a fascinating example of how old family lines in Cape May never seem to let go. I am beginning to wonder why anyone in Cape May even bothers to make out a will.

OPPOSITE AND ABOVE: The old Reeves Homestead on Stevens Street.

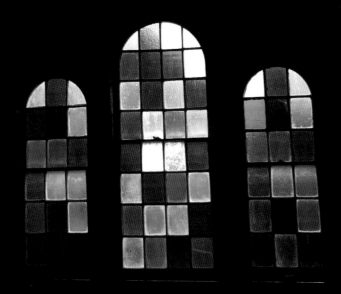

WHEN MY COUSINS Jon and Virginia Mangano bought the old Cold Spring Chapel on Jonathan Hoffman Lane they did not realize they were inheriting a few long term tenants. The old chapel, now a private residence, was built in 1884 on land donated by Nathan C. Price. It was used as an overflow space and Sunday school for the Cold Spring Church. When the canal was built in the 1940s, many buildings were either condemned by the state or moved to new locations. The chapel was moved to the site of what was once a two room schoolhouse, which its present location. When Price Hall was built, the chapel was sold to a Mormon group and later became a private home. The ghosts never left.

People over the years have reported seeing three young girls sitting on the front steps of the chapel. They disappear as quickly as they appear. I have sensed several children in the building. The feeling I receive from them is that they find the building "safe." Since it was a chapel, they feel "protected" from any bad energies. Ghosts taking refuge in a church, but still stuck on Earth—such irony. Do these children like it where they are? Could they cross over to the Other Side if they wanted to go? More to come on this supernatural Sunday school in *Book 4*.

OPPOSITE: The old Cold Spring Chapel. ABOVE: Inside the chapel—light in the darkness.

The John F. Craig House

S O MANY GHOSTS, so little time. This is the way I always feel when I stay at the John F. Craig House on Columbia Avenue. Not that the house has that many ghosts, it's the neighborhood that keeps on barging in!

I have spent many weekends here in the past couple of years with fans of the paranormal who want to spend a night in a real haunted house. Each of these special weekends is a joint effort between myself and Barbara and Chip Masemore, owners of the Craig House. The highlight of each paranormal weekend is a séance in the parlor each Saturday night. The neighborhood ghosts have yet to disappoint and sometimes they even let the house ghosts have a chance to squeeze into the mix!

I am not sure why I seem to be able to draw in so many local ghosts when I channel here. It could be that this section of Columbia Avenue is quieter than other sections of town, and more paranormally active. For some reason, when I slip into a trance with a group at the Craig House someone always seems to come through, bringing with him lots of icy cold spots and a few dead friends as well.

The Craig House's first owner, George Richardson built the main, front part of the house in 1866 and moved the rear, older section from another location in town to add on to the back of the house. Richardson tragically drowned off the coast when his boat was tossed in rough seas. He had sold the property in 1870 to B.K. Jamison. Philadelphia Banker and Industrialist Benton Knott Jamison owned the house for twenty years until his company, B.K. Jamison, went bust in 1890. Jamison, a friend of several U.S. Presidents, had been known to throw his wealth around in Cape May by hosting wild and extravagant parties at the house.

John Fullerton Craig (pictured left) a wealthy Philadelphia sugar baron, bought the house from a financially stressed Jamison in 1891 and used it as a summer getaway for his family. The house stayed in the Craig family until the 1950s. John Craig, his second wife Emma Craig and a few other phantoms call this cozy Bed & Breakfast home.

Just because you're dead, doesn't mean you don't deserve a vacation at the beach.

ABOVE: Ghost Host John Fullerton Craig. OPPOSITE: The John F. Craig House on Columbia Avenue.

68

OPPOSITE: A side view of the Craig House. ABOVE: Hostess with the Ghostess Emma Camp Craig.

The Mason Cottage

EDWARD A. WARNE has been spotted walking back and forth from his old summer home on Columbia Avenue to the ocean many times. Of course this is nothing unusual, with the exception that he is dead. Which is nothing unusual for Cape May.

Wearing his trademark top hat and carrying a cane, Warne is one of the most frequently sighted ghosts in town. His daily sojourns to the beach demonstrate just how similar a ghost's "life" is to the life he had when he lived.

His home, now The Mason Cottage B&B is a great place to stay if you love to be near the ocean and enjoy all things Victorian. The classic mother-daughter house was actually built by Warne as a "father-son" house. He gave the eastern half to his son John as a wedding present. All was fine until the grandchildren came along and started to wreck Edward's side of the house, at which time he did what any loving grandfather would do. He had the doors between the two parts of the house bricked up.

To this day it is felt Warne enjoys "his half" of the house along with his ghostly servant, Florrie. Room service in the afterlife—you gotta love Cape May.

71

Angel of the Sea

W HEN WILLIAM WEIGHTMAN, Sr. wasn't busy cornering the market on quinine or real estate, the head of Powers and Weightman was spending his summers relaxing in Cape May. Of course back then, his cottage (mansion) was just at the beginning of its busy trip around town, and it was still in one piece.

Today the Weightman Cottage is two separate buildings called Angel of the Sea, one of Cape May's top Bed & Breakfasts. Built before the Civil War, around 1850, on the piece of land on Franklin and Washington that is now the post office, the Weightman Cottage was, and still is, one of the showplaces of the town.

It is hard to tell just who is haunting this old building. In 1881, Weightman's son had the house moved by mules to the ocean front. The workman hired had to cut the house in two to move it and, when it arrived on Beach Avenue, they realized they could not put it back together, hence the reason it is two buildings now. The houses were moved again in 1963 to their present location on Trenton Avenue.

I have always felt this was a "have ghosts, will travel" story. If you were a ghost and still residing in your old home and someone started moving it to another location, wouldn't you follow right along? If a haunted dwelling burns down, and is later rebuilt, ghosts may come back and haunt the new structure. If you move a haunted house, you are moving the ghosts right along with it. Someone is attached to this old mansion, and to date I have not been able to ascertain who that ghost may have been. When a house has a long history, the hauntings may be a mystery.

OPPOSITE and ABOVE: Angel of the Sea, Bed & Breakfast on Trenton Avenue.

Circa 1875 - Dr. Ware's Drugstore was on the first floor, Ladies of the Evening worked on the 2nd Floor and Gambling was enjoyed on the 3rd Floor. The old saying here went: What you won on the third floor, you would spend on the second floor and then go to the first floor for a cure.

ABOVE: Dr. Ware's Drugstore circa 1875. (Courtesy of Doug McMain)

A HOUSE MAY CHANGE OWNERS, and a building may change businesses, but don't expect the ghosts to change. Being stuck on the Earth Plane has done nothing for them in terms of motivation.

Ghosts are an imprint of the person who lived. Pharmacist in life, pharmacist in death, even if the pharmacy is now a clothing store. The same goes for anyone who haunts Cape May. Since there is no reason to have to work, other than sheer boredom, ghosts will stick to routines from their lives. In the case of the House of Royals, the two ghosts named Margaret and Terry still follow old *traditions*.

Can ghosts see each other? Do they interact with each other? I would say yes to both questions.. So what do these ghostly ladies of the evening do for a living? Well, maybe the word *living* is a little inappropriate, so let's just say they keep busy in the afterlife.

The Queen Victoria is one of the top five Bed and Breakfasts in Cape May. It is run by a highly professional staff — dead and alive — that will make your stay memorable and have you coming back for more. My first experience with the ghosts was on the second floor was when three times in the same evening someone knocked at our door. Each time I would get up to check to find no one in the hallway. On the third time, I put out a psychic line and realized the ghost was carrying a tray of drinks. Remembering this was a gambling and "entertainment" facility in the 1800s, I thought I may have been experiencing a residual haunting, an image from the past stuck in the air. Then the ghost started to communicate with me, asking me if I would like a cocktail. If only they were invisible! I said, "No thank you," and she left. For some reason the ghost recognized me as a ghost. Was she tuning in on my psychic energy? It was a wonderful experience, I just wish the bar had closed a little earlier.

Circa 2009 - The Queen Victoria's House of Royals Bed & Breakfast. Fabulous guest rooms on the second and third floors, a few long dead Ladies of the Evening, and unfortunately no gambling.

I think these *ladies* worked exclusively on the upper floors. Dr. Samuel Fithian Ware, who had the pharmacy on the ground level, was a prominent doctor, and I doubt he would have been involved in a prostitution ring. He was also married to Colonel Henry Sawyer's daughter Elizabeth Eldredge Sawyer. I wonder what his father-in-law thought of the little business venture upstairs?

Speaking of Henry —

77

NATIONAL HISTORICAL LANDMARK

The Chalfonte Hotel 1876

The Magnolia RESTAURANT Public Welcome

301

The Chalfonte Hotel

COLONEL HENRY SAWYER began building the Chalfonte Hotel on Howard Street in 1876. He was the first to call in the alarm when flames began shooting out of the Ocean House Hotel across town at the beginning of the Great Fire of 1878. Sawyer's Chalfonte was spared by the flames, and the great hotel stands to this day.

I had been trying to track down the ghostly maintenance man at the Chalfonte for many years. I had sensed him about the hotel, fixing this or that, but could never get a close enough fix on him to find out his name.

My friend Annie Mullock remembered a man who tended the furnace and was a caretaker at the Chalfonte many years ago. She seemed to agree with me that he or someone like him is haunting the old building — as well as keeping an eye on it. We never *really* retire.

Activity like this could be a ghost's delusional way of thinking he was still alive and refusing to let go of what he no longer had — life. On the other hand, there could be some form of physical construct in which ghosts exist. If a ghost is a mirror of his or her Earthly incarnation, maybe everything in nature has a "ghost." The ghosts might be existing in a world identical to ours, but physical only to them. A parallel dimension. A mirror.

Colonel Henry Washington Sawyer (1829-1893)

I have recorded ghosts saying, "I am going to vacuum," and "Let's go eat." Taking these recordings at face value, one would think that ghosts actually consume food or that they are standing on a rug that they can see is dirty and needs cleaning.

At the Chalfonte I have sensed two distinct ghosts. The first is the maintenance man who roams the long corridors of the Chalfonte, checking for anything in need of repair.

The second ghost I found sitting high up in the cupola, watching sorrowfully toward the ocean. In her arms she held a baby. I could see her and the baby clearly in my mind's eye. Both looked "alive" and well. The lonely young woman did not acknowledge me. She kept staring out to sea, as if waiting for a husband or loved one to return from a voyage. She had radiant blue eyes and longish chestnut hair. I think she and the child died soon after she gave birth. Did she stay at the Chalfonte? Was she a servant? At first I thought this was a residual image, but soon after I arrived she stood, turned, walked right through me and left. She was consumed by her own feelings, and they were keeping her Earthbound.

Ghosts stay behind for a reason. She was waiting for a love, and a father, to return. I don't think he ever will, and she'll keep waiting anyway.

OPPOSITE: The Chalfonte Hotel. ABOVE: Col. Henry Sawyer (from *The History of Cape May County* by Lewis T. Stevens, 1897)

The Stockton Row Cottages

MANY YEARS AGO, when I went on one of the walking ghost tours, we always stopped in front of the row of identical cottages on Gurney Street near the beach. The tour guide would mention a story about a ghost cat at one of the cottages and we would then move on. Each time I took the tour I wondered which of these cottages was *really* haunted — by people. Since these homes were built opposite what was once the mammoth Stockton Hotel, hundreds of people have lived in these cottages. Someone had to still be lurking in the ethers.

Then one day I had the opportunity to meet Bob and Jennie Mullen. The Mullens had just purchased #26, called The Belvidere Cottage. Off I went with my tape recorder and psychic senses switched on to full power.

ABOVE: The 1871 Stockton Row Cottages. OPPOSITE: #26 The Belvidere Cottage.

The Belvidere

WHEN I ARRIVED at the Belvidere Cottage I was greeted by one of the former owners who was in the process of carrying wash up to the second floor. The woman had a little trouble walking, and I would have helped her carry the laundry up the stairs—if she wasn't dead.

I was soon joined by another man who insisted I tell the Mullens, who had just purchased the property and were in the process of fixing the place up, that some of the plumbing needed to be fixed and a door was sticking, etc., etc,.

It seems that some ghosts never tire of watching over their former dwellings. After thinking about this encounter and later learning that Edward Warne (who is haunting the Mason Cottage up the block) built and owned some of these cottages, I began to realize I may have encountered Warne again, this time at another location. If he had built and rented some of these cottages and still remains here in the afterlife, he may in fact still be acting as a ghost landlord.

When ghost tales like this take on such breadth and detail, they start to make us think they border on the fantastic, but ghosts are only human beings that keep on ticking after death. Why wouldn't we follow in our old footsteps in the afterlife? I wonder where I'll be haunting.

Jackson Street is one of the oldest...

Postcards of Jackson Street looking north 1904 and 1907 — Same old buildings...

and most haunted streets in Cape May.

Same old people — they just happen to be dead now — and they make great ghosts.

JACKSON STREET is more haunted than not. Not every house on the street has a ghost—but who's counting? It is a toss up between Jackson Street and Columbia Avenue for Most Haunted. At the moment, I would have to give the edge to Jackson Street as the paranormal heart of the city.

On the right are three of the more well-known haunts in town, The Saltwood House is in the forefront, followed by Windward House and The Inn at 22 Jackson. The Saltwood and Windward share a ghost. The Inn at 22 has one of its own.

As I discuss at length in *The Ghosts of Cape May Book 1,* there has been a story going around about a ghost named Esmeralda who haunts the turret suite of the Inn at 22 Jackson. Her bedroom was in the tower, and she had a special servants' door that lead to a small back staircase behind her bed. She apparently was beloved by former children of the house, and to this day plays phantom board games with guests. STOP. Sometimes ghost stories can be passed down from generation to generation and like the old game of telephone, get more convoluted as time goes on. In this case, the first story was just that—a story.

There was no one named Esmeralda, there is no bed or secret door in the turret of this house, and the only ones playing games are the people regurgitating this folklore. Former family members who lived in the house in the 1950s made the story up for a friend who worked for a Philadelphia newspaper.

After spending a few nights here and thoroughly investigating this haunt, I realized there was no one by the name of Esmeralda in residence. There is however a ghost. I psychically picked up her name as Anne, maybe Roseanne. She does like to play with younger children, but not with board games. Instead, she throws a ball around in the house—if you are in the mood to play.

OPPOSITE: The Inn at 22 Jackson (L) Windward House (C) Saltwood House (R)

ABOVE: Katherine Loftus Campbell (1873-1964)
(Courtesy of Walt Campbell)

When the Saltwood House was built in 1906, local realtor Charles T. Campbell and his lovely wife Katherine were the first to move in. The Windward House had been built a year earlier by a financier from Philadelphia named Baum. The story that has been passed down by the owners of the house was that Katherine Campbell was Baum's mistress, and he moved her in next door. Katherine is thought to haunt between the two houses. The story has yet to be substantiated and so far, Katherine is keeping silent on the issue.

83

Centre House CAPE MAY, N. J.
Destroyed by Fire 1878.

J. HENRY EDMUNDS (tall guy with the dark mustache to the right) was always a man about town. Still is—just dead. When the old Centre House Hotel on Jackson Street and Washington Street burnt down in the 1878 fire, Edmunds bought part of the rear property and moved three buildings to the site to create a new residence for himself and his family. Today that home is The Merry Widow Guest Suites on Jackson Street.

The Merry Widow is one of my favorite places to stay. It is like stepping back in time. There were rumors for years that a young girl haunted the third floor suite of the house and that she was the granddaughter of J. Henry Edmunds. Unfortunately, Edmunds and his wife, Georgianna Hand Cummings Edmunds (pictured right, next to Edmunds) did not have any grandchildren. Their three children died

ABOVE LEFT: The old Centre House Hotel. (Courtesy of Don Pocher)
ABOVE RIGHT: J. Henry Edmunds, his wife Louise (left of him) and his telephone exchange staff. (Courtesy of Walt Campbell) OPPOSITE: The Merry Widow.

as infants. So the story of a granddaughter haunting the house is out. Someone in that house does *not* like thunderstorms, and occasionally doors will be heard slamming upstairs when a storm approaches.

I have recorded voices of an older man, Edmunds I think, and a younger woman, in this house. I do not think the two ghosts are related. During one of the recording sessions, I was sensing the name "Karen" and on tape, right before I say that name Karen, an EVP is heard saying the same. It is one of the few direct correlations between a psychic communication and EVP recording that I have documented. I psychically heard "Karen" as the voice recorded on the tape. No one else present heard a woman's voice say Karen prior to listening to the playback of the recording. To date, we do not know of a Karen who lived in the house. She may be a transient ghost.

Someone like J. Henry Edmunds, who was a mover and a shaker in town, in his day, would have a strong connection to this Earth Plane. In the late 1800s he owned shares of every major utility in Cape May City, served twice as Mayor, worked with land speculators trying to redevelop the old Mount Vernon site and even bought the Cape May Ocean Wave to use the newspaper as a political tool to espouse his Democratic Party views in a mostly Republican community.

Edmunds was so involved in Cape May politics and business that I don't think he can let go. Ghosts stay for some reason. Two of those reasons are strong material or emotional attachment to a place

or person. As far as I can tell, J. Henry Edmunds never left. When someone builds an empire, they rarely want to let it go. What does one do with this Earthly power as a ghost? Haunt the local newspaper office? Hmm—there's a thought. There just happens to be a James haunting the old Star and Wave offices, now CapeMay.com. I wonder...?

OPPOSITE: The Merry Widow on Jackson Street.
ABOVE: The final resting place of James Henry Edmunds' body.

The Carroll Villa Hotel &
The Mad Batter Restaurant

91

T HE HISTORIC Carroll Villa Hotel is the venue for one of Cape May's *mirror ghosts*. Ghosts are rarely seen, and
when they are, it is usually in a wispy or shadowy form. As I slept in one of the guest rooms at the Carroll Villa, I
awoke about two in the morning to notice a strange shadow shifting back and forth in the mirror above the dresser.
Checking the opposite wall, I could not find anything that should have caused that reflection. In the blink of an eye,
I turned again to look at the mirror and saw the face of a young woman with long, stringy hair with pieces of debris stuck in it.
It is safe to assume she drowned. She said nothing, just stared at me for a moment, then faded into the shadows of the mirror.
I laid awake for almost an hour waiting for her to return. She never did.

93

RIGHT: Looking up Jackson Street with the Carroll Villa in the foreground.

John McConnell House

ABOVE: The John McConnell House on Jackson Street

IN 1882, when John McConnell was running Ebbitt House, which would later be called The Virginia, I am sure he had no idea that he was setting up a permanent residence — and I do mean *permanent*.

This beautifully restored private home was built on the site of another hotel, destroyed in the Great 1878 fire. While I have sensed the McConnells at the Virginia (see the next spread) it is the ghost of a small boy, and a former servant who haunt McConnell House. One messes, one cleans.

Very little is known about the McConnells. Alexander McConnell, either John's father or brother, owned a good stretch of property on this side of Jackson Street prior to the Great Fire. If these ghosts have anything to do with the McConnell family, it has yet to be determined.

Before I knew anything about the hauntings here, I had told the owners that a small boy had been hiding under the house. He was an orphan and apparently for this child, the space under the house was good enough to be his new home.

Ghosts of children are more likely to reside in places like this. They seem to be out on their own and being dead is one long camping trip in the wild for them. However, this young lad does make forays into the house to take a nap every now and then.

When I explained my findings to the owners they confirmed that in one of the bedrooms on the third floor, they would make the bed to return a short time later and find the covers messed and an impression in the mattress — just small enough to be that of a child. Luckily there is a ghost maid to go along with the kid.

95

The Virginia Hotel

W ANT TO PISS OFF A GHOST? Try calling it by the wrong name all the time. Some of the staff members at The Virginia Hotel have not heeded my advice to start calling the original owners (pictured above) by their correct names. The two giant portraits that were found in the cellar during renovation of the hotel in the 1970s are (I think) Mr. & Mrs. John McConnell. One of the former managers not only referred to them as "Mr. & Mrs. Ebbitt," but also said that Mrs. McConnell looked more like a Mr. — McConnell.

A short time later I got a call from someone who worked at the hotel. It seems that Mrs. McConnell had enough and threw herself off the wall, crashing to the floor! Luckily the giant oil painting and frame were not badly damaged. I do think these two haunt the hotel. They have been watching over their old property since the late 1800s. The Virginia Hotel is one of my favorite haunts, an if you ever need to find me in Cape May, I will usually be enjoying some of the great food and wine, and talking to dead people. Not necessarily in that order.

OPPOSITE: The Virginia Hotel on Jackson Street. ABOVE: Early portraits thought to be the hotel's first proprietors. 97

Poor Richards Inn

CAPTAIN GEORGE HILDRETH was another one of those "men about town" in the old days. He was involved in many different business enterprises and ran the first lifesaving station in Cape May. In addition to his farm and home by Cold Spring, Hildreth built himself a summer cottage in Cape May. After the Great Fire of 1878 wiped out all of Jackson Street, Hildreth had a new summer home and the Carroll Villa Hotel built on the site of his former hotel, the Wyoming Cottage.

George Hildreth's first wife Sarah died shortly before this new cottage was finished. George searched for a second wife to take his side. One of the ill-fated beaus he took to court for breach of a marriage proposal! I have yet to come across George Hildreth, but his second wife is another story. Exactly who the second Mrs. Hildreth was is unknown at this point. First I was told her name was Beatie, short for Beatrice. However, I could not find the body of a Beatrice Hildreth in Cold Spring. So I contacted Annie Salvatore who, with her husband Joe, runs Historic Cold Spring Village and lives in George Hildreth's other house. Annie told me the second wife was listed as "Mary A. Hildreth" and rumor has it that Mary did not like the first Mrs. Hildreth at all and disposed of her personal belongings after marrying George.

The woman haunting Poor Richards is, I think, the second Mrs. Hildreth. If the first Mrs. Hildreth hung around as a ghost in the old house, the second Mrs. Hildreth would not last very long there once she joined the ghost realm. Luckily for the Hildreths, they had enough houses to go around.

Ghosts are the people they were in life. Our likes, dislikes and personalities never die—like it or not.

THIS SPREAD: Various shots of Poor Richards Inn on Jackson Street.

99

ABOVE: Joseph McMakin's (seated with the cane) Old and New Atlantic Hotels just before they burned in the 1869 fire. (Courtesy of the Craig Family)

The End of Jackson Street

AT THE TERMINUS of Jackson Street two long lost hotels once stood, the Atlantic and the New Atlantic. These two buildings were two of the first boarding houses or hotels in Cape May.

Brothers Benjamin and Joseph McMakin came from Philadelphia and got into the hotel business. They first purchased the old Atlantic (in the picture to the left) and when business began to boom they bought the tract of land from the beach going back along the east side of Jackson Street all the way to Washington Street. In 1842 they built the four story New Atlantic, which was the first hotel in Cape May to be painted.

The landscape has since completely been redesigned in this part of Cape May. Even buildings like the Baltimore Hotel and the King Cottage, which stood on this spot after the New Atlantic was history, are now gone themselves.

One of the questions I am often asked is, "If someone is haunting a building and it burns down, does the ghost move into whatever is built on that spot?" Would the McMakins still be around Cape May if their old hotels were burned and gone? Possibly.

I wanted a cover for this book that best represented both Cape May, Cape May's long history as a resort and Cape May's ghosts. When I spotted this picture hanging in Toby and Rona Craig's family room, I knew I had found something that spoke volumes. A picture can speak a thousand words and in this case that picture can also represent a thousand ghosts.

Something like a fire will not send Cape May's ghosts packing off to Baltimore or Philadelphia. They cope and they adapt. It is very seldom that a ghost is haunting a specific building. The ghost just happens to be residing in that building at the time. If the building goes away, the ghost moves in somewhere else. Old ghosts never die—they just change their addresses.

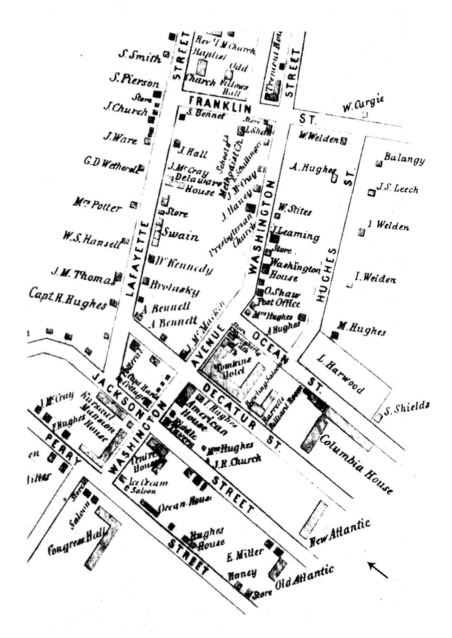

ABOVE: The arrow points to the part of the 1850 Numan Map inset of Cape Island (Cape May City) where the cover photo (left) was taken in 1869.

W E'VE BEEN PROGRAMMED by the Hollywood film industry to think of ghosts as malevolent, shadowy phantoms intent on getting us to join them. To understand what ghosts really are, one must remove the Hollywood factor, take a deep breath and calm the imagination.

Ghosts are the people their bodies left behind. That's all. Yes, some ghosts can see us and interact with us should they choose, but most ghosts are trying to work things out about their own past lives and do not need the living annoying them as some kind of sport.

My good friend Tom, who is a psychiatrist, often uses the catch phrase, "It's always about you, isn't it?" Human beings tend to think this way. We think ghosts are always trying to haunt *us*, that they are trying to deliberately scare *us* or communicate with *us*. With ghosts, it's rarely about us. It's usually about them.

A sliding chair, phantom footsteps above, an air conditioner turning itself on and off and adjusting its own temperature are a few of the ghostly goings on I have experienced at Columbia House. It's easy to think William Essen, the house ghost and a former confectioner and baker in town was trying to get my attention but, in fact, he was probably just going about his daily business when this meddling psychic got in the way. I admit a microwave display changing from a time to "Hello" is a bit odd, but hey, he did run a bakery so what's strange about talking through an oven for a baker? Perhaps he was just being friendly to me, in a ghostly sort of way.

OK Tom, so maybe occasionally it *is* about me. Just ask the ghosts, they'll tell you.

LEFT: A chair or a ghostly baker sitting in a chair?
OPPOSITE: The Lovely Columbia House Guest Suites.

Hannah McCrea's House

GHOSTS CAN SEE PEOPLE, but people rarely can see ghosts. Cats, it is suspected, can see both people and ghosts and can develop a like or dislike of their ethereal house mates.

On Perry Street there is an old house now called The Seahorse. It is a private residence that has been beautifully restored by its owners Donn and Holly Kirk. In the house's early history it was owned by John and Hannah Eldredge McCrea.

John McCrea was killed in the battle of Williamsburg at the young age of 28 and his widow and children lived in the house for many years thereafter. Hannah McCrea is still there, and while she does not "live" any longer, her spirit still enjoys the comfortable surroundings of her old homestead.

While John McCrea is long gone, Hannah has a few new friends to keep her company, and they are not humans. Ouba, the Sphynx (seen to the right) and his cohort Spanky, are the house's two feline tenants. Soon after I did my first investigation of this house and determined it was indeed Hannah McCrea doing the haunting, I made my way up to the bedroom that may have been Hannah's when she lived and is now hers in the afterlife.

Ouba and Spanky joined us shortly and started to prance around the bed and began to watch something in the room. They were both focused on the same spot. Later that

night, after I had left, the cats had disappeared. Don was alone in the house and went searching for them, only to find they had been locked in the bedroom. The only way this could have happened is if someone had shut the door on the cats once they had entered the room, but no one was home at the time who would have done that. No one but Hannah that is. I think the old girl just wanted a little company.

While Hannah resides peacefully upstairs, a more intense spectre has been seen on the first floor. Holly and Don's daughter Erin was brushing her teeth in the downstairs bathroom (above) one night. She was alone in the house and had the bathroom door behind her open to the downstairs hall-way. As she glanced up into the mirror she spotted the weath-ered face of a middle aged man glaring at her from behind. She turned to see who had entered the house and he was gone.

The man who gave me the name "Carl," was not attached to Hannah McCrea or her family, at least I didn't have that feeling at the time. Most of the property surrounding the house up to Washington Street was originally the Mansion House, a huge hotel owned by Richard S. Ludlam. I think Carl may have come from that time period. Carl comes and goes from the house while Hannah "lives" quietly upstairs. Is she waiting for her husband to return from the war, so long ago? Every ghost has a reason for staying. Hannah has no comment.

ABOVE: The bathroom mirror where the ghost appeared. RIGHT: Ouba the Sphynx.

The Bacchus Inn Cottage

COOKING A ROAST for 70 years may seem as implausible as can be, but to a ghost, that roast may seem as medium well done as me.

Some ghosts move about town and go about their daily business, while others are *really* stuck in one routine. One of the ghosts who haunts the Bacchus Cottage either really likes to cook, or is a residual haunting in the true sense.

When the previous owners of this house had called me in to tell them about their unseen spirits, I detected a woman with the name of "Conwell." As it turned out, Fanny Conwell had owned the house in the 1930s. At the same time I was getting an image of this woman along with this name. She was heavily engaged in preparing something in the area of the downstairs that at one time was a kitchen.

Ms. Conwell was complaining aloud that the roast was overcooked again and blaming an unseen oven on the nefarious deed. I tried to communicate with her, but she continued to pine about the lost roast.

When something traumatic or emotionally intense happens in one's life, it may leave an imprint of that event on the spot it occurred. I am not equating burning a roast to a major life upheaval, but if this occurred during the Great Depression when money was tight, losing a roast could have indeed been a very big deal.

Phantom footsteps are also heard in the upstairs reaches of this old house, now part of John and Lisa Matusiak's fabulous Bacchus Bed & Breakfast duo. I have communicated with the ghost of a woman who called herself "Mrs. Mason" on the second floor of the house. A transient ghost, she told me she stayed here after she lost her property in the Great Fire of 1878. While Fanny Conwell may indeed be a residual haunting, a continuous tape loop that neither interacts nor changes behaviors, Mrs. Mason was much more communicative and willing to indulge me on her past life in Cape May. Communicating with a ghost like this is done with the mind, not verbally. Mrs. Mason's energy was vibrant and made me feel good. She was like meeting an old friend at the shore and having a reunion. It could well be Mrs. Mason who wanders up and down to the third floor at night. Many, including myself, have heard the phantom footsteps, clunking up the winding stairs and then coming back down, late at night.

It *is* possible that Fanny Conwell, or whoever that ghost is who's cooking the roast downstairs, is not a residual haunting and is, in fact, a real bona fide spirit. Some ghosts refuse to believe they are dead and cling to something they were doing when they died. They run through the same exercise over and over again, as if it gives them some credibility to still being alive. Other ghosts will recognize they have died and begin to live out a new "life" in the afterlife. Every ghost is different. Some ghosts may eventually even decide to cross over to Heaven.

As for you Mrs. Conwell, give it up dear, the roast—and you—are both quite dead. It's time to move on to a new life somewhere else. You're just lucky smoke detectors don't come back as ghosts. They'd be playing your song 24/7.

The Linda Lee B&B

THE MOST FASCINATING THING about ghost investigating is the absolute randomness. One may think he or she knows who is haunting a house, but unless a thorough investigation is done, one might as well pull names from a casket, or a hat should there be no casket available.

Ghosts can be former owners or family members of a home. In Cape May they could be former tenants, servants or none of the above. With such a concentration of ghosts in one town, the spectral inhabitants of America's oldest seaside resort also like to move around. Cape May is after all, a seaside vacation spot and even dead people like to mix it up a bit. Do *you* stay in the same vacation place every time you go away? If you answered yes, you are probably doomed to become a ghost. Just kidding.

The Linda Lee is owned by my friends Archie and Stephanie Kirk, two of the most forward thinking, personable B&B owners in town. They also own the Bedford Inn on Stockton Avenue, another great place to stay.

The EVPs that I have recorded at the Linda Lee were baffling to say the least. Alone in the dead of winter, sitting in the downstairs guest suite, I ran a tape. I sent out a psychic "join me" followed by a verbal invitation. The ghosts did not disappoint. On the tape, two ghosts are heard conversing, not with me, but with each other. They mention *vacuuming* the room and going out to *eat* — two things you do not expect a ghost to be doing!

Did I record a bleed-through from another time? Were these words being spoken by living people and somehow they were slipping through time and space to be recorded on my tape recorder? Or do ghosts really eat and do things as mundane as cleaning or vacuuming?

Could the Ghost Realm be a physical construct somehow attached, but separated from our own? There are so many unanswered questions about ghosts and hauntings. Every time paranor-

RIGHT: The old servants' staircase to the attic.

109

mal research gets a step closer to the answers, something baffles the equation and sends it three steps back. To our limited intelligence, ghosts are still not tangible. They exist, yet they evade our mental grasp. What are they really?

My friend Gerry Eisenhaur, who sometimes comes along on my ghost investigations and acts as my technician, brought in his gauges, probes and recording equipment one night to the Linda Lee. As a psychic medium I rely on my own internal equipment first, but I think it's important with ghost investigations to combine many different techniques and take from the composite outcome the most conclusive and satisfying evidence. With ghost investigations, one needs all the help he or she can get!

At the Linda Lee, as I called the ghosts to join us in the second floor hallway near the front window of the house, Gerry had set down a EMF meter on the floor in a doorway to one of the guest rooms.

First we heard the soft, creaking steps coming down from the third floor, next a cold spot swirled in and around us. Finally, the meter started to spike, more than it ever had before. I asked the ghost to step back from the meter and it went to zero. Next I asked them to step over the meter, and it spiked again. We repeated the exercise three more times with similar results. By combining my psychic abilities with Gerry's scientific equipment we were able to accurately measure a ghost!

Soon after, the ghosts retreated and the hallway warmed back to room temperature. The meters went quiet. The ghosts were gone. Had they deliberately tried to help us or did we just happen to get lucky and stumble onto their path? This was a great experience for all of us. The idea of making such a strong connection was exhilarating. It was almost as much fun as staying at this great Bed & Breakfast and enjoying life by the sea with the living!

LEFT: The Linda Lee B & B. RIGHT: The Linda Lee's vintage parlor.

The Jacob Leaming House

EVER LOOK UP at a window and see someone staring back at you? What if you looked up at a window of a house you knew was vacant and someone was staring back at you—and the next second they were gone?

Some ghosts mind their own business and ignore the living. Some ghosts make it a favorite past time to watch us. They have us at a distinct advantage because while they know exactly what we are doing and where we are going, we rarely know the same about them. It is very seldom that a ghost—in this case referred to as an apparition—is ever seen.

Luckily with ghosts there are *always* exceptions to every rule. At the Jacob Leaming House on Columbia Avenue, I have received numerous reports of passersby seeing someone or something watching them from the upper windows of the old house.

While the Memucan Hughes-Colonial House still gets first prize for ghost sightings in windows, the Jacob Leaming House is a close second.

My friends Audrey and Bill Schwab, who own this house, have a great sense of humor and are wonderfully open to the whole ghost/haunted house thing. I am not sure if they picked this house or the house picked them!

Two ladies, Hannah and Rachel, haunt the house. We have not been able to trace them to the Leaming family who built this house in the 1860s, but we think they may have been servants of the family at one point in time.

It is these ladies who have been seen by Bill and Audrey's daughter and who have made frequent "curtain calls" in the upper windows. The ghosts here stay on the third floor. Many ghosts retreat out of the way of the living, and Bill and Audrey rarely use the upper floor for themselves. The ghosts' energies in this house are very strong and of a positive nature as are 99.9% of all hauntings. It is the living who have the monopoly on negative energy!

What makes a ghost visible to the living? My theory is that ghosts with stronger energies and personalities can create all kinds of physical phenomena. Most likely, manifesting in visual form is difficult for a ghost.

We see ghosts with our minds, not with our eyes. Ghosts somehow project their images and those of us who are "sensitive" are able to view this projection. This is why a few members of a group may see an apparition, while others see nothing. In most cases, an apparition will take on a shadowy or wispy form and appear transparent. In more extraordinary examples, a ghost may briefly appear solid and human, only to be discovered when they suddenly vanish in our presence. At the Jacob Leaming House, the girls have the guest (ghost) appearance thing down pat—they may even wink at you.

ABOVE: The Magnificent Southern Mansion

The Southern Mansion

GEORGE ALLEN bought a large tract of land from William Corgie in the 1850s and built his large and fabulous summer cottage that he called "The Southern Mansion."

Allen's mark is all over the old place, now a fabulous Bed & Breakfast, on the edge of the downtown and across the street from the haunted Washington Inn Restaurant. The only thing Allen did not leave here was his ghost. Contrary to years of legend, it is not Allen or his niece, Esther Mercier who haunt the house. The current chain rattling is being done by a sweet little old lady named Mary Crilly.

Mary was a wonderful old gal who was loved by friends and neighbors and lived into her 90s in the old mansion. Crilly's husband Daniel had given the house to Mary as a wedding present in 1946. Daniel died and then their daughter Maryanne soon passed of cancer.

Borders Mary had taken in began to see ghosts and Mary assured them they were benign. On one occasion, Mary questioned a tenant about what the ghosts looked like and as the person described what he had seen in an upstairs hallway, Mary produced a picture of a man and a younger woman. They were the same people the tenant had witnessed as ghosts—they were Mary's husband and daughter.

As Mary became old and frail, and the property went into arrears for back taxes, a few relatives decided she and the house should go. The property was sold and Mary was put into a nursing home. Her wish that she could die in her house would not come true.

Luckily for Mary Crilly, she lived (and died) in Cape May. Upon passing, she made a beeline right back to her old mansion where she reunited with her husband and daughter once more—and died happily ever after.

ABOVE: Original owner George Allen (Courtesy of The Southern Mansion)

115

The Emlen Physick Estate

CAPE MAY'S ORIGINAL HAUNTED HOUSE is, I am happy to report, still haunted. Dr. Emlen Physick and his two happily dead maiden aunts, Emilie and Bella, continue to enjoy their old homestead on Washington Street which is now a museum run by the Mid-Atlantic Center for the Arts (MAC.)

The house is one of the few haunted mansions in the country that is accessible to anyone who dares pay it a visit. Sure there are other mansions in the country and world that are haunted, but very few that are *this* haunted are open to the public on a regular basis.

Each Halloween, I take a group into the house for a "Midnight at the Physick Estate" event. This house is usually the most active late at night when everyone else (living) in the neighborhood has gone to bed. While the ghosts here have been known to take off and leave me standing in the dust, during the first Midnight tour they put on a floor show. Footsteps and voices in the upstairs bedrooms above us, a phantom baby crying, doors opening and closing, banging on the walls, and a Victrola playing an old record (there is no such instrument in the house) made for a paranormally exhilarating evening! The following year, Midnight was much more subdued. Had the ghosts amused themselves enough with our group and my psychic sleuthing?

Dr. Physick has been making his presence more known to me over the last few years. At first it was only his Aunt Emilie and Aunt Bella lurking in the shadows. Now the good doctor himself has begun to make appearances. Emilie Parmentier (above)

was very close to her nephew Emlen Physick in life and that bond continues in death. From what I have learned of Dr. Physick I think, even if he had crossed over, he would come back to check on his favorite aunt and his old homestead. Perhaps he never crossed over. The three of them, Emlen, Emilie and Isabella could have all chosen to stay behind after death. I think we have that choice in the end, cross over to Heaven or tend to unfinished business.

This house has really only had one family living there since the beginning, now all dead, but still dwelling in the house. Emilie was the last to die

ABOVE: The Emlen Physick Mansion as it appeared in the late 1800s. That's the beach and ocean in the background! (Courtesy Mid-Atlantic Center for the Arts, MAC)

in the family and left the house and property to her neighbor and friend, Frances Brooks. Dr. Harry Sidney Newcomer and his wife, Dr. Marian Newcomer, purchased the house around 1946 from Brooks. Dr. Marian died in 1949 and Dr. Sidney married his assistant in 1955. They lived in the house for a couple of years when, according to people who had known the Newcomers, the couple moved into an apartment downtown because the new Mrs. Newcomer was afraid to live in the house—since she felt it was haunted.

Seems like Dr. Physick and the girls didn't take long to start haunting the old place!

Dr. Physick was also a huge animal lover. A perennial bachelor, he was always seen arm in arm with one of his furry canine friends. His mother, Mrs. Frances Ralston was not an animal lover and would not allow the dogs in the house, now that she is gone I think Emilie, Bella and Doc have established an open door policy for the ghostly pups. I have sensed dogs in the house on several occasions when I have been investigating inside the home. Cats are place centered, dogs are people centered, and these dogs are sticking with their old master! I haven't run across dog ghosts in Cape May with the exception of the Emlen Physick Estate.

MAC and I have developed several tours that run throughout the year in which you can visit this great old haunt for a haunted house experience that is *up close and personal*. I suggest paying a visit to the Physick Estate soon—the Doctor is currently *in*.

ABOVE: Dr. Emlen Physick and friend. (Courtesy of MAC)

HISTORICAL CAPE MAY.

MOUNT VERNON HOTEL.

JOS K. HAND

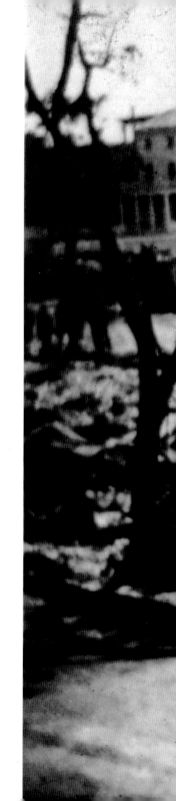

On September 5, 1856, after closing down for the season, the mammoth Mount Vernon Hotel, which sat on the beach just west of Cape May proper on what is today the cove, went up in flames. Inside the huge structure, Philip Cain, part of his family and their housekeeper quickly burned to death.

The story is in all of the history books about Cape May. The hotel was not yet completed and was having some financial difficulty. It was the largest hotel in the world at the time. The sections were one quarter mile long and the dining room could seat three thousand people.

I had sensed ghosts in the vicinity of the hotel when I walked the cove. I never quite knew if it was the Cain family or some other spectral remnant of old South Cape May, the neighboring borough that washed out to sea. I never really gave it much thought, after all, the building was long gone, and I am not fond of investigating open space. It gets rather boring.

Then something changed. Someone wanted their story told and they started to reach out to me through my West Cape May friend Barbara Morgan, who happens to own a haunted home on Eldredge Avenue.

Barbara's ghost is a boy named Andrew. One night, while we were both IMing each other on the computer, I started getting psychic messages repeating over and over again. They kept saying they were for Barbara, that the "Andrew" we were looking for had something to do with Mount Vernon. We have been trying to figure out who Bar-

FIRE HAS A WAY of bringing out the best in ghosts. They seem to react to dying in flames as though they just took a dip in the water. After getting through the horrific physical transition from flames to death, it seems many ghosts simply get up and move on. Not that they are psychologically unscathed; they are affected by the trauma. However the fiery ordeal does not always buy them a fast ride to the Other Side. Rather the opposite. It seems to create souls who refuse to be suddenly deprived of their beloved lives.

Cape May has suffered through several tragic fires. Luckily, no lives were lost in either the 1869 or the Great 1878 fires. One fire, however, did take its toll of human life and a few of those souls still haunt the town in which they burned.

OPPOSITE: The 1869 fire started in the mall and then burned out part of Jackson and Perry Streets (Courtesy of Walt Campbell)
ABOVE: The Great Mount Vernon Hotel that burned in 1856 is a suspicious fire. (Courtesy of Don Pocher)

bara's ghost Andrew is and where he fits in the history of her property. At first I though the message was that he was *from* Mount Vernon, New Jersey. Soon they started saying fire and giving us more clues. It was not Mount Vernon, a town. It was the *hotel* Mount Vernon. Barbara and I began digging online to see what we could find. She found *The New York Times* article talking about the fire and the deaths, the same story that is in all of the Cape May history books.

Nothing was clicking, so we let it drop. The next day Barbara emailed me to say she had uncovered another article in the following Monday's (9/9/1856) *New York Times*. 1856 was a long time ago and it seems one of the most interesting parts of the old story was lost all of these years — until now.

Philip Cain's teenage son, *Anderson* perished in the fire along with two sisters, Martha and Sarah. Anderson's brother, Philip Jr., made it out of the hotel, badly burned, and was taken to the United States Hotel. Philip Jr. lived long enough to tell the authorities what had happened. Anderson had jumped out of the second story window to escape the flames. The fall broke both of his legs, and he suddenly became engulfed in fire and could not run. He died at the foot of the hotel. His brother died the next day at The United States Hotel on Washington Street.

The article continued to explain that a disgruntled employee, an Irish woman who worked for the hotel that summer, had arrived earlier in the day demanding owed back wages. Cain was short on funds at that point and sent the woman away. The woman made threats to Cain that she would retaliate. These threats were heard by several other people in town. That night, as the Cain's slept, the hotel mysteriously went up in flames. The woman was arrested, but released for lack of evidence.

I wondered what this had to do with Barbara and her house. Then we found a connection. The Cains lived in Vincentown, New Jersey where Barbara keeps her horses. Had a ghost hopped a ride to and from Cape May with Barbara? A stretch.

My psychic wheels began to turn. Something sounded so familiar about the victims in this story. I checked my notes and found a sentence just too similar to pass by. In my notes from The Ugly Mug, I met a young man's ghost called "Danny." Danny said he died jumping from a building and breaking both of his legs. At the time I thought he worked on a building and fell. Could Anderson Cain have been called "Andy?" Did I psychically get the names wrong or was it just a coincidence?

Prior to the Ugly Mug building, there existed a large boarding house called the American Hotel (pictured left, behind the horse cart) on the same spot, run by the O'Bryan sisters. Across Decatur Street from the American Hotel, in the spot where Atlantic Books now stands, was Tomkin's United States Hotel (see the picture on the next page.) Both buildings were lost in the 1869 fire.

Anderson Cain is listed in the *New York Times* article as "Barkeeper, aged 20." The fact that he was a bartender makes the idea of him haunting the Ugly Mug even more plausible.

While I was working to finish *The Ghosts of Cape May Book 3,* I decided to investigate the Atlantic Books store on the mall. Atlantic Books in situated

OPPOSITE: A vintage photograph of Washington Street circa 1860 looking towards Congress Hall. (Courtesy of Walt Campbell)   123

in a former bank building on the corner of Washington and Decatur, directly across from The Ugly Mug.

As I was channeling in the cellar of the book store (right) I began to sense a younger man coming into my psychic view. He was very interested in what I was doing, but did not talk very much. Eventually a ghost dressed in a watchman's or policeman's uniform arrived and chased him away. He then left abruptly himself. Was this boy possibly Anderson's younger brother Philip Cain, Jr.—who died in the United States Hotel which stood on the very spot as the book store? A possibility, but it could also have been one of a hundred other ghostly kids in town.

Then the mystery began to unveil itself. As I was sitting writing this story, I was staring at the building (on the left) and remembering my original investigation of the Ugly Mug a few years back. I checked my notes to see if I might have mentioned the name "Anderson" or "Andy." As I read the old story again, I did a double take and a chill ran down my arms and legs. In that investigation, I had identified two ghosts near the bar that night—Phil and Junior. The owners of the Ugly Mug at the time remembered two patrons by that name who had passed, so I thought nothing of it—until now. Phil

United States Hotel CAPE MAY, N. J.   Destroyed by Fire Sept., 1869

and Junior. Anderson's brother was *Philip, Junior!* Had I mistaken one ghost for two? Could that ghost have been trying to give me his full name, Philip Jr.? All the facts started lining up—a young man, a former bartender, jumping from a building, breaking his legs and dying.

Of course, this is just another ghostly scenario, but it was certainly starting to look like the cast in this haunting had changed. Is Danny really *Andy?* Philip and Junior, Philip Jr.? We may never know.

If it is the Cain brothers who have been haunting their old neighborhood all this time and a forgotten newspaper article is finally shedding some light on this old mystery, I wonder if the rest of their family has stayed with them or moved on. The boys wouldn't be too lonely if they hadn't. They have plenty of ghostly company on the mall.

OPPOSITE LEFT: The Ugly Mug today with the old Kennedy Pharmacy building (now The Cotton Co.) across the street.
ABOVE: The United States Hotel built in 1849 by A.W. Tomkins of Philadelphia. (Courtesy of Don Pocher)

Ghosts of the Mall

IN THE LATE 1800s, the Washington Street Mall was not a mall at all. It was Cape May's Main Street USA. Horses and carriages replaced the pedestrians we have roaming the area today. Not much has changed since those days (see the picture on page 122) with the exception of a few more stores, a few less horses and a lot more ghosts. Our first stop is one of the oldest buildings.

Dr. Kennedy's pharmacy was located across from where The Ugly Mug now stands in the building that is today occupied by Lace Silhouettes and The Cotton Company. This has always been one of my favorite haunts because the children who haunt this shop have such positive energy. I don't know who they were in life. The only information they gave me were their names, Albert and Caroline, and the fact that they were not related in life, but have adopted each other in death. Many ghosts form an "afterlife family" which is no different than if someone went away to college, made new friends, and those friends became an extension of the family. Most people who are hanging around as ghosts have lost their families. Their loved ones have crossed over and probably did not think to look back to see if they had left anyone behind—as a ghost. This is *my* theory at least.

When a former manager called me in to investigate, she had all kinds of paranormal stuff happening. One thing that kept occurring was a bathroom sink turning itself on. Remembering that Civil War hero and Chalfonte Hotel owner, Colonel Henry Washington Sawyer who dropped dead in that bathroom (he was at the pharmacy for something for his upset stomach which turned out to be a massive heart attack,) I thought for sure I would run into one of Cape May's famous departed. As it turned out, Colonel Sawyer was not haunting the building. It was the handy work of two mischievous children—Caroline and Albert.

I first found the ghosts in the old basement of the building where they had taken refuge near a hot water heater in the winter. What struck me as interesting is that ghosts needed warmth. We think ghosts can drain energy from power lines and appliances, but heat? If they have no physical body, why do they require warmth? What are they warming? Or is this just a throwback to when they were alive and could somehow sense the warmth? They told me they felt safe in the old cellar, at the bottom of the ancient wooden stairs. They were just glad to have a home.

ABOVE: The Lace Silhouettes and Cotton Company building today. OPPOSITE: The ancient stairs leading deep beneath the old pharmacy building.

One of my best ghost interactions in Cape May was in the Lace Silhouettes section of this building. The managers had asked me to come in and do a book signing. At the time they were selling huge amounts of my books — and they were a lingerie store!

I had set up a table underneath a rack of brassieres. It was one of the strangest book signings I had ever done. Between signing books, I was making small talk with some of the ladies who worked in the store. There were one or two customers who were shopping at the time. We started talking about the strange occurrences with blue garments in the shop. Caroline was very fond of anything blue and the manager would often find blue garments pulled off the racks and thrown on the floor in the morning.

As I joked to the manager that she should put up a sign that read "Caroline recommends these blue dresses," there was a crash on the other side of the room. No one was near the spot at the time. When we checked, a rack of *blue dresses* had been *ripped down off the wall, hardware and all!*

We all witnessed it happen. No one had been near that side of the room. The metal bar that was holding up the dresses was ripped right out of the wall, pulling part of the wood with it. It was right on cue.

If ghosts do not have physical bodies, they should also not have a set of ears. So how do they hear us? It was obvious to me that this girl and boy *did* hear me and quickly acted out my words. How do ghosts hear what we speak? Are they reading our thoughts — or do they exist on that other plane, what I call the *ghost realm* in some kind of energy form that gives them back their senses, including the *sixth sense*.

Next time you do some clothes shopping here, should you pick up something blue. You might take home more than you bargained for. Talk about a *buy one, get one free!*

WHEN I INVESTIGATE a building for ghosts, I try to ignore the surroundings. The building may have absolutely nothing to do with the ghost who is haunting. Like the living, ghosts are transient beings and their sense of real estate ownership may become compromised by their death. Ghosts may eventually feel pushed out of their former living space and move on to another building. Some ghosts are also associated with an earlier, long forgotten business that existed in a building or family who had lived at a site in the distant past. Ghost investigation even gets more confusing when the haunted dwelling is new construction and the ghost is tied with a former, now extinct, structure that once occupied the site. When ghost hunting, don't let the current surroundings fool you. Looks can be deceiving. At the new Winterwood Christmas Gallery, the ghost is definitely not Jacob Marley or any of his *Christmas Carol* friends. Although, like Marley, this particular ghost may also be watching every penny.

OPPOSITE AND ABOVE: The new home of Winterwood, the former New Jersey Trust and Safe Deposit Company.

129

Ghosts have a way of keeping their own energy close to the vest, I have a lot of trouble reading paranormal energy from outside a haunted house. I need to be within close range to get a good take on what may be haunting inside. Remember, when it comes to ghost hunting, looks can and will be deceiving, and one of the biggest traps I see amateur ghost hunters fall into is getting caught up in the "atmosphere" of a haunt.

A house can *feel* haunted because it *looks* haunted, not because there is an actual ghost. We have been brainwashed by too many haunted house movies over the years. The atmosphere and decor of an old house can create ghosts in the mind of the observer very quickly. Don't let your imagination get the best of you if you plan on going ghost hunting!

When I investigate for ghosts, I sit and close my eyes to try to "see" if there are any ghostly presences. I use my psychic senses and mediumistic communication to seek and find. I look past the scary Victorian furniture or darkened cellars or attics. This concentration exercise became necessary because of my ADD (attention deficit disorder.) I just could not stay focused if I kept my eyes and ears on the living and tried to search for ghosts at the same time. Who knows, maybe my ADD is what actually made me psychic. I am always mentally drifting off somewhere else. Perhaps this disconnect allows me to make contact with another plane of energy more easily? Sounds good anyway. Imagine someone with ADD trying to focus in a giant Christmas shop, filled with all things glittering, sparkling, blinking and playing music!

I had never really paid much attention to this building when it was an art store. Once Winterwood moved in, I was visiting on a regular basis because they carried my books. I stopped in to autograph the copies and check stock. There was always "a feeling" or a twinge of the paranormal hovering in the ethers here, but nothing substantial. The blinking and jingle-belling in this store pulled my attention in all directions like salt water taffy. That changed when I went upstairs.

One of the managers had asked if I would check to see if there were more copies of my books in an upstairs cabinet. I obliged and climbed the long staircase to the top. I gazed down over the store and thought how interesting it was that there was an upstairs part of the Christmas shop that I had never noticed. As I turned and opened one of the drawers to check for my books, I heard one of the ladies come up the stairs behind me. Next there was a slight tap on my shoulder and I assumed she was going to tell me I was looking in the wrong place. I spun around to find no one was there.

It's a large building and sounds do echo. The footsteps could have come from downstairs. Then I heard someone whistling up on the second floor with me. It was all around me, but nowhere at the same time. I could not tell the tune as it was there one minute and gone the next. I also noticed the sounds coming from the busy store below had quieted for a moment, as if everyone was listening to the sound. I peered over the railing and looked below. All appeared calm and the ambient noise returned to normal. It was at that moment that I began to see flashes of a man in uniform, a police officer

OPPOSITE: A Ghost's View of the new Winterwood shop.

officer with a night stick. It was an image in my mind that looked like someone walking down a long hall lighted by a strobe light. Since the building clearly stated on the facade that it was originally a bank, I assumed this was the ghost of a former guard. Was this a real ghost or had I experienced some sort of bleed-through or warp in time? Had I psychically stumbled upon some stored bit of imagery, embedded in the ethers of the building, that showed me scenes from another time—called a residual haunting?

Some paranormal investigators feel that bleed-throughs are what ghosts are all about. Theoretically, in certain energy situations one would be able to peer through a "psychic window" and see the same spot, but at another time.

Others think ghosts are people from other dimensions or universes that are bleeding through to our own universe. I surely hope not. I really don't see myself writing *The Aliens of Cape May Book 1*. Ghosts are much more fun.

Several of the staff members at Winterwood have told me they have sensed a ghost in the new location. They should be well trained—they had years of experience at the *old* location up the mall!

For years the old Winterwood shop (left) on the mall was reputed to be haunted. Even the locals can't remember how far back the haunting stories go or when they started. The Winterwood employees told me they saw a man in a white smock, floating through the back storeroom. They also heard women talking and laughing. Boxes and ornaments would mysteriously be knocked off shelves, only to be picked up by an employee and then fall off again.

The man in the white smock is thought to be one of Cape May's former dentists, Dr. Henry Loomis, who kept an office

in back of this building. The ladies are thought to be the Knerr sisters, the last generation of the Knerr family to tend the dry goods business (above) at this location.

I could never sense the Knerr sisters here. They may have been upstairs (which I have never investigated) or they may have been out. Maybe I wasn't their type.

The good doctor, however, is another story. At one point I was doing a little trance channeling in the side alley next to the shop, and I sensed a strong image coming at me down the alleyway. It was an old dentist in a white smock chasing three or four ghostly children. I could hear their screams. I assumed (hoped) they were playing a game of tag. The dentist had an old drill, sound and all, with a long frayed wire hanging from it. He seemed to be almost floating after them. The image was as much comical as it was frightening. If this *is* the ghost of Dr. Loomis, he *really* needs to retire!

OPPOSITE: The former Winterwood location on the mall.
ABOVE: The Knerr family ran a dry goods store at the site from the late 1800s until the 1950s. (Courtesy of Walt Campbell)

134

AS I MENTIONED in the Merry Widow story, the house was built on part of the old Centre House Hotel property. Closer to the mall, on that same original piece of land, at the corner of Jackson and Washington Streets, stands the old Capital Hotel and Bar building, seen left.

Today this building houses shops including Fralinger's Salt Water Taffy (one of the best sources for almond macaroons in Cape May!) Upstairs above Fralinger's is also one of the best sources in town for ghosts.

For many years, some of the employees at Fralinger's used the upper floors of the building for storage. Some of them have encountered a ghost they affectingly named "Gunthar."

After investigating the old hotel rooms in the upper reaches of the building (pictured right) I had determined the ghost to be named "Henry," not "Gunthar." This was a psychic determination, a feeling conveyed by the energy of the ghost. Henry's energy felt like it was fading away—it was definitely not strong. He lead me to believe that he had once stayed in the hotel with his wife, and perhaps he had died there. She moved on. He never checked out.

My partner, Willy, had snapped a series of pictures while I was investigating upstairs at the old hotel. One of the most interesting should please all of you "orb" fans out there. When I made contact with Henry, dozens of orbs, those tiny balls of

light, appeared in one of the photographs. There were no orbs in any of the other photographs. There is light coming through the window over the door behind me, and the door does have a shiny finish, two things that could contribute to a flash bounce and create orbs.

In an old building like this there is also dust kicking around. That dust could have been stirred up by my walking up and down the hallway, and the particles may have refracted the flash. Orbs are *very* controversial and ghosts are rarely seen.

OPPOSITE: The Capital Hotel circa 1910 with Frank B. Wrisely's bar on the first level on the corner of Decatur & Washington Streets. (Walt Campbell)
ABOVE: Craig searching for ghosts in the old Capital Hotel building, surrounded by "orbs." (Photo by Willy Kare)

SOME PEOPLE in the energy working field have told me that ghosts are drawn to my mediumistic energy like a moth to a flame. I have also met a ghost who seems to have been drawn to flames as well!

Jackson Street is one happening paranormal spot. If Cape May had a "ghost enclave" this would be it. At the point that Jackson Street crosses the mall, it is called "Jackson Mountain," being a whopping 14 feet above sea level! This street was also an old Indian trail to the ocean, paved and surveyed in the late 1700s as one of "Cape Islands" first roads. Layers of history, lots of ghosts — usually.

When the little shop on Jackson Street pictured right was a candle shop called "Flimm Flamm," the staff had some very unusual experiences after hours. Each night when they left they would extinguish any candles they had burned during the day when the shop was open. They would lock up and leave for the evening. Upon returning in the morning, some of the candles would be burning once again.

When I visited the shop in its next incarnation as Wildberries, which has since moved next to the Whale's Tail, I sensed a shorter-framed man sitting up on the old staircase, smoking a pipe. It is interesting that a ghost would or could still be smoking a pipe. The pipe was as transparent as the ghost. After we die, do we continue to "live" somewhere else and does our new life stay somehow linked to our former life? Do ghosts exist in a state that is another physical dimension like ours?

Then there is the issue of relighting a candle. Ghosts seem to have the ability to move objects, and they can affect electrical circuits, but lighting candles? I suppose if a ghost can smoke a pipe it could light candles in our world as well.

The man on the stairs seemed like he had been in the tiny house for years. I was never able to trace the history of this building. When Valerie Sperlak had Wildberries at this location, she had done some renovating and uncovered an old trap door in the floor in back. She opened it for me one day, and I felt a surge of psychic energy surround me. Had we found something's hiding spot? I was not about to *light a candle* and venture down to find out!

ABOVE: An old ship's bell hangs with the ghosts in the mall. OPPOSITE: The former Wildberries building on Jackson Street.

GHOSTS FOLLOW the lifestyle they had when they lived. This is why ghosts (generally) haunt where they lived and not where they died. The next time you are at the mall, take a look up. You will suddenly notice lots of darkened windows and possibly a few ghostly figures staring back at you.

Lined up shoulder to shoulder like a wild west *ghost town,* the old buildings on the mall are not only storefronts, they also double as living space. Above each store is usually an apartment and *some* of these dwellings are haunted.

The ghost of a child haunts my friend Dan Casale's apartment above the Shoe Rack, next to the Ugly Mug. The child's ghost, who calls himself "Michael," seems to be another ghostly orphan in town. No parents, no family, just a young boy trying to find a place to call home. Michael is very drawn to Dan's cat, Soup. Cats are thought to be able to see ghosts. The way Soup carried on some nights in Dan's apartment, something must have been trying to get the cat's attention!

The child's ghost was witnessed by several people including Dan, walking through the apartment late at night and vanishing into the wall. Ghosts are rarely seen, but this young ghost has the energy to manifest an image, albeit a shadowy one.

The ghosts in these upper reaches of the mall are trying to continue their existence on the Earth as best as they can without a physical body. Something is keeping these souls tethered here, stopping them from crossing over to Heaven. Each one has a story, and most of these souls are benevolent.

Ghosts' lives cannot be easy. We should try to view our unseen friends with a little compassion. You never know, they may someday turn out to be *your* neighbors.

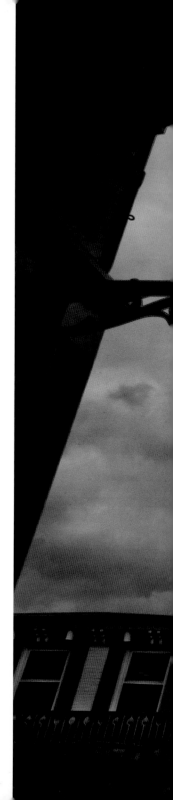

W HEN YOU BUY your tickets for our ghost trolley tours, you will find yourself standing in front of one of the smaller haunts in town. This old ticket booth originally came from Fairmount Park in Philadelphia. It was used by the Fairmount Park Guards, since the 1870s, as a Guard Box. Today, the Mid-Atlantic Center for the Arts (MAC) uses this old booth to sell tickets for their various tours. Since I am partnered with them on all of the ghost trolley tours in town, I often find myself standing by the structure.

There have been times, especially in late October when the nights can be cold and dark, and the mall is deserted after 7 PM. I have been standing around the ticket booth signing autographs after one of my Halloween trolley tours. Once the last tour is finished, the trolley usually takes off and leaves me in the darkness of the mall. I sometimes wind up talking to a few tour-goers near the ticket booth.

It has been on these quiet nights, after the doors and windows have been closed and locked for the night that I have thought I have seen and heard someone in the booth,. I remember one late night in October, as I was finishing my bottled water and snack before starting back to where I was staying, I had leaned up against the booth to adjust a sock. Someone inside the booth said very firmly, but in soft voice, "Yeah?"

My first reaction was to respond, "Hello?" My second reaction was to hightail it back to my B & B. Alone at a haunt is one thing, alone in Cape May — at a haunt — in the dead October is a bit much for me. After I had written this story in *Exit Zero* newspaper, someone emailed me to tell me that when the booth was in Fairmount Park, a guard had been shot and killed inside. While I don't think that is who is doing the haunting here, trauma leaves its mark on a spot, even if that spot happens to be moved around. Someone is haunting this booth. Go buy a ticket and find out.

Enough shopping for ghosts on the mall — let's go to the beach and take a plunge six feet under!

RIGHT: The Mid-Atlantic Center for the Arts' (MAC) ticket booth.

142

HOUSES are not the only places ghosts haunt. If I were a ghost, I would just die having to be cooped up in the same old house everyday. If I were a ghost in Cape May, I would be haunting the beach—and I would not be alone. Cape May's beaches have changed over the centuries, losing ground to the battering tides and storms. The once great dunes that lined the oceanside beaches during Colonial times are gone, and the beachfront dwellings have changed with time as well. All this change means little to a ghost. Landscapes change, ghosts adapt. In Cape May entire boroughs have washed into the ocean—houses, beaches, elephants—all gone. The ghosts just keep on haunting, and strolling along the shore is still a favorite pastime of the dead.

OPPOSITE: Beach Avenue in Cape May.   ABOVE: "Old Jumbo" the wood and tin elephant that stood in now lost South Cape May in the 1880s. (Walt Campbell)   **143**

The Old Light at Cape May Point

ANY LOCATION can be an active haunt. Ghosts usually haunt where they lived, however, sometimes a traumatic or quick death causes ghosts to become stuck near the spot where they died. Sometimes ghosts also gather at a central location in an almost communal sense. The Cape May Light is a perfect example of a centralized haunt for many ghosts, old and young, long dead and recently departed. This area gives "go to the light" a whole new meaning!

Lighthouses were vital in the old days to keep ships from running aground and to help them navigate the coastline. The remains of Cape May's first 1823 light and second 1847 light are now far out in the surf under water. The current light was built in 1859 farther inland from the 1847 structure to protect it from the encroaching sea.

People ask me quite frequently, "Is the lighthouse haunted?" My answer is, "When the ghosts are inside, it surely is." A house is only haunted when the ghosts are at home, and that rule goes for lighthouses as well.

For many years before the first lighthouse was erected at Cape May Point, shipwrecks were a common event. Privateers, our early pirates, would intentionally lure ships close to shore on dark, moonless nights by hanging lanterns around their horses' necks and walking them to and fro on the beach. To a ship at sea, this ploy created the visual effect of other ships safely sailing closer to the land. The ships' Captains would usually follow suit, not realizing they were being lead into a trap. Once the ship was grounded, small pirate boats would encircle and eventually board the ship. Armed with

weapons, this assault could end with the crew of the stranded ship either being thrown overboard, beaten or killed. Should a person die this way, his ghost would most likely try to come ashore. From the density of paranormal activity at Cape May Point, it seems quite a few ships and their crews were lost near the tip of the peninsula.

Legend even has it that Captain William Kidd, the famous English pirate, hid some of his treasure near Lily Lake. To this day it has never been found. I have often walked around the lake and tried to call up some ghostly help for treasure hunting. Unfortunately, one of my shortcomings as a psychic is not being able to get the right lottery numbers; the other is not being able to find buried treasure. At least I can talk to ghosts.

Besides a few ghostly privateers looming around the light, there is a rather diverse group of phantom figures, including several jumpers from the days before the catwalk at the top of the lighthouse was fenced in. Of all these ghosts, several stand out in the paranormal crowd.

OPPOSITE: The 1859 Light - ABOVE: Drawing of a wreck off the Cape May shoreline in the 1800s (Author's Collection)

In the beginning of the 1859 light's history there were several buildings surrounding the base of the light. The oil storage building and one lightkeeper's house are extant today. While vandals burned down one of the houses in the 1960s, the other is now used for the Park Ranger's quarters. This old house seems to be the home of a former lightkeeper's wife and the meeting place for some of the ghostly children of the area. This is what I would call a centralized haunt.

Should you happen to be walking up the winding 199 step spiral staircase on a hot summer day and feel an icy breeze zip past you, there is no need to be alarmed. It's just the dead lightkeeper's dead wife.

The ghostly woman seems to be carrying pails of either water or oil up the steps to the top where she vanishes. I ran tapes inside the lighthouse, late at night when the grounds have been closed to tourist traffic and the surrounding area is quiet, I have captured quite a few *A*

Class EVPs inside the structure. "A Class" EVPs are almost as clear as a human voice and can be heard without having to use headphones. One of these EVPs had a woman yelling at two children to come to her. The response added a chilling dynamic to this haunt.

The child cried out, possibly knowing I may be able to hear his voice, "Help me, please — I don't want to go with her!" It was not the reaction of a child to a mother, rather the response a child would give to a stranger trying to take him away.

Inside the lightkeeper's cottage more children's voices both appeared on the tape and came to me psychically, including a boy who gave us an address as to where he died. It was a nearby street on the point, but we could not find the exact number. All of these children seem to converge on the lighthouse grounds. They didn't all die there. They come there

ABOVE: An old postcard of the Cape May light showing the keeper's houses. (Author's Collection)
OPPOSITE: Birdseye view from a lighthouse portal and the light and cottage today.

in a communal way to play and socialize. Boys will be boys and girls will be girls, and that goes for their ghosts as well. Some of these children seem to have drowned, while others died of childhood diseases.

One child talked to me about being injured on an old, rusty fence and getting sick. When he got better, he said, his family had gone. His family may have been vacationing in Cape May when he died here. They may have taken his body and left. So many ghosts in Cape May are just the orphaned souls of children, lost to play by the sea for eternity.

Cape May Point wraps around to the west and eventually meets up with Sunset Beach. The ghosts here move around. I have sensed some of the same spectral personas at both the lighthouse and at Sunset Beach.

Sunset Beach and the Sunken Ship

CONTRARY to what you may think, the old concrete ship *Atlantus* or the pile of rock that's left of it, is *not* haunted. Ghost hunting is as much about weeding out folklore and overactive imagination as it is about finding a real ghost. Our unseen friends are usually found where we least suspect them to be.

So many ghost leads are "dead ends" that I try to wait for several reports of one location to come in from different sources before I set off to investigate. When one is trying to investigate on open land, or open beach in this case, searching for ghosts is like finding a dead seamstress's needle in haystack.

One of the more interesting things I enjoy doing at Sunset Beach (besides having lunch at the snack bar and looking out at the bay) is to sit quietly and close my eyes on the beach and go into a light trance. Luckily, at the beach if you are sitting with your eyes closed, no one notices.

The energy here is very intense. It is a good energy, and I cannot say for sure whether all of the quartz crystals we call Cape May Diamonds are creating that energy or not. Many energy healers and psychics work with crystals. The various stones are thought to enhance and focus energy to be used or read by the handler. Remember the old crystal ball? Maybe Sunset Beach is one big magnifying glass into the past.

I have seen images of carriages coming to and from the water's edge. This was the site of one of the first steamboat landings in the 1800s and Sunset Boulevard was the main drag into town where the hotels were located. These images could be residual, but a few of the people I have encountered seem much

more real and interactive than a tape loop of residual energy. I have seen what looks like bathers in old fashioned dress hanging around the old changing booths that were built from pieces of the Atlantus. There is also a ghostly man and his darkly colored dog. Many have spotted these two ghosts. I have sensed the man was drowning and his dog went in after him, and they both perished. Truly sad, but at least they are still together.

OPPOSITE: Sunset Beach and the remains of the concrete ship Atlantus. ABOVE: The old bathing house.

149

Congress Hall

LUCKILY FOR CAPE MAY, some of our most historic buildings can take a beating and keep coming back. Congress Hall Hotel was first built in 1816, near the foot of Perry Street by a man named Thomas Hurst Hughes. It was called the "Big House" for its shear size compared with everything else on "Cape Island" at the time. The hotel eventually garnered the nickname of "Tommy's Folly," as the locals thought Hughes was crazy to open such a large hotel on such an isolated and sleepy peninsula as Cape May was back then.

The 1816 structure burned in 1818 and was again rebuilt in 1819. In 1826 Hughes and his wife, Lydia, sold the building to Samuel Richards who in turn sold it back to Jonas Miller, who had an earlier structure on the site in 1812. Miller then turned over ownership to his son, Waters Burrows Miller.

It was the younger Miller who greatly expanded what was then called Congress Hall (named in 1828 in honor of former Congressman and owner Thomas Hurst Hughes.) Waters B. Miller added an immense wing in 1854 creating the L shape that the current incarnation mimics today. This version of Congress Hall was the largest of its type, stretching back to South Lafayette Street and down Perry Street almost to the water with the two wings shadowing the great lawn in front of the hotel facing the ocean.

The Great fire of 1878 claimed 35 acres of prime Cape May real estate, including Congress Hall. The hotel was rebuilt in a smaller scale, and this time from brick instead of wood, in 1879. That hotel still stands today. This piece of land has layers of history and quite a few permanent guests—I mean ghosts.

My first ghost encounter here was with Congress Hall's long dead proprietor, Jonas Miller. It was during the period that the hotel was undergoing a major renovation and the building was closed down at the time. Calling himself only "Jonas," he lead us to the dark and, at the time, truly spooky cellar where he implored us not to let anyone hurt "Smitty."

At first I thought that Smitty was a beloved pet, but soon we found an old boiler plate (pictured left) that read "Smith Twin Tubular Boiler Co." It seems even after almost 200 years, Jonas Miller was still keeping the place going. Now *that's* dedication! There is always some reason for a ghost to be hanging around: emotional attachments, material attachments or even the love of a place where one once lived. Sometimes souls just do not want to let go of something they love. Cape May seems to be one of those places that gets a hold on us and keeps bringing us back—living or dead. Jonas Miller and a few of his ghostly friends love staying at historic Congress Hall. Who wouldn't?

ABOVE: The boiler plate from Jonas Miller's old hotel boiler. OPPOSITE: The 1879 version of Congress Hall.

151

ABOVE: A view of the sea from one of Congress Hall's many balconies.

When the Mid-Atlantic Center for the Arts had their Museum Shop on the ground floor level of Congress Hall, they reported all kinds of ghostly activity. The shop sold vintage reproduction toys and childrens' books, which on certain mornings they would find scattered about the floor. Nothing had set off the alarm during the night, but *something* had been playing with the toys. A particular doll and book were repeatedly found on the floor, favorites no doubt of the spectral young children.

I have sensed several ghosts of children in and around the hotel for many years. As I mentioned, boys will be boys and girls will be girls and even if they are dead, they still love toys and games.

There is a pattern to most hauntings and that pattern usually tells a lot about the person or persons doing the haunting. When things are being "played with" and toys and dolls are moved around without anyone touching them, it is most likely the work of a child's ghost. In the 1800s in Cape May, about 60 percent of mortalities were children under the age of 10. That's a lot of dead children to cross over to Heaven. Cape May is like a proverbial class trip for these children. Like may school outings, someone always manages to get lost. Many children haunt Cape May — and they are having a great time doing it!

ABOVE LEFT: Craig searching for ghosts on the upper floors of Congress Hall. ABOVE RIGHT: The former Congress Hall in 1869, before the great fire took it down. 153

The Parris Cottage

JONAS MILLER has it made. Not only does he have a beautiful old home, just a block from the beach, but he is also only half a block from work. Talk about an easy life. Of course, being dead helps.

When Miller arrived in Cape May from his birthplace of Port Republic, NJ, he built a small framed hotel in 1812, near the ocean about a block south of Perry Street. In 1816, he built a larger structure nearby and sold it to Thomas Hughes. Eventually Miller and his son Waters Burrows Miller bought the property back sometime in the 1820s and ran it for many years. Actually, Jonas Miller is still running the place, but you won't find him there at night. After work, he returns to his old homestead on Perry Street, around the corner from Congress Hall. Ghosts follow lifelong patterns.

For many years this house was called the Parris Cottage, but before that it was Jonas Miller's house. The house is presently haunted by two ladies who may or may not be related to the Miller family.

One of the women comes through strongly and seems to have owned the house in the 1890s, the other could be one of Miller's daughters or a servant

from his household. Whoever they are, their presences can be felt by many. These ladies also produce the best ghostly footsteps that I have heard. A group of us were investigating the downstairs parlor when we all thought we heard other people walking around on the second floor. No one else was in the house except us.

Phantom footsteps are a common sign of a haunting, yet ghosts do not have physical bodies. Something is creating impact to make the sounds. Do our souls have a body of energy that mimics a real body in size and shape?

OPPOSITE: The Parris Cottage on Perry Street. ABOVE: Jonas Miller (1785-1869 But don't tell him that.) (Courtesy of Jack Wright)

The Sea Villa

A CENTURY BEFORE Atlantic City's famous slot machines were plugged in, gambling was in full swing in Cape May. In the late 1800s, gentlemen would come to Cape May to enjoy the seashore and roll the dice. Many of our historic buildings like the Queen Victoria's House of Royals, The Mainstay, The original Blue Pig and The Sea Villa were legal gambling establishments in Cape May.

The Sea Villa, with its magnificent view of the ocean, is one of the last of the small gambling hotels still standing in Cape May. While gambling these days has been reduced to playing Monopoly in the sitting room, the hotel harkens back to the 1800s and a much simpler time. Like the House of Royals, this haunt also features of few (dead) former Ladies of the Evening hanging about.

One of the most interesting ghosts here is Irene, who I think is the same Irene (Wright) that is haunting the Macomber. Miss Wright, according to those who knew her, wore loads of perfume in her day. Phantom floral scents still waft through the air here, and I think Miss Wright is one of the ladies doing the wafting. Although she was *not* a "Lady of the Evening" like the others. She was a visitor to town and she loved Cape May. In life she stayed at many different inns here. Death has not slowed her down. Just ask her.

OPPOSITE: The Sea Villa on Perry Street

The Ocean View Hotel

VICTOR DENIZOT BUILT his new Ocean View Hotel directly on the spot of his old hotel that burned in the Great 1878 fire. He eventually built the Lafayette Hotel next door when business began to grow. The Lafayette has since been torn down and replaced with a more modern structure, but the old Ocean View still stands like a sentinel on the beach, welcoming tourists to its wonderful bars and restaurants and welcoming ghosts coming in *from the ocean*.

After investigating this old building a few times over the years, I started to sense something more to it than the pretty Victorian trim and quaint seaside appeal. Psychically, the building had a rumbling of energy, like one feels at a busy train station, but in this case it was the feeling without all of the trains and crowds. It was this dull roar of unseen people that convinced me to trance channel on the upper floors one night.

The local ghosts here are a woman named Julia, who may have also worked as a seamstress in town. Julia has a connection back to the Denizots' time. There is a ghostly bartender that I call "Gilbert," who says very little psychically and only sends me imagery that he used to tend bar here. Julia is very active in this building and her energy has been very conducive to creating EVPs on tape. Julia definitely watches over everything that happens here. She is completely in tune with what the living are up to. She can also move physical objects with ease, including the chair you see on your right. Some ghosts are barely perceptible, others are right in our faces and interact with the physical environment just like we do.

As for the crowd below, either this building or this location attracts souls who were lost at sea. I can only tell you what I see with my psychic perception. In this case something here is like a lighthouse for the dead at sea. Do those souls who die at sea

ABOVE: The paranormally powered chair at the old Ocean View Hotel

water need assistance from other souls? Ghosts seem to look out for each other, especially the newly deceased. At least if they can't get right to Heaven, someone is throwing them a lifeline. Maybe this is how it really works—ghosts could just be souls left here on the Earth Plane to help the freshly deceased to let go and move on to Heaven.

For some reason Julia also feels the need to rearrange furniture around the upstairs office area. A small chair was found by several employees in front of a door on the third floor. No one is quite sure why she does this. A theory is she had a young child who kept running out of the building, and this was her way of making sure he or she stayed put in a room upstairs.

Julia has strong energy and is that type of ghost who can move physical objects like chairs and, in her case, small objects like canned goods and boxes. Some of the wait staff have experienced these phenomena in the storage room on the fourth floor, where various items stored on the shelves come flying off for no apparent reason.

Julia also has found a way to manipulate electrical circuits. Ghosts, being fields of energy can interact and change other fields of energy just as one person can push another person out of the way. The staff has told me that when things get busy and one of the servers is not doing a good job taking care of customers, the lights in the hallway will start to flash. Electricians have checked these circuits and even replaced the switches to no avail. Julia will have her say, with or without a voice.

And speaking of a voice. If you want to try your hand at recording EVPs, bring a tape recorder with you and come have a drink on a slow night at Martini Beach. Set the recorder down on the table in front of you and hit record. Ask a few questions, leave time for the ghost to answer. On playback, you just may be surprised what you hear.

This ghost likes flickering lights, moving chairs—and enjoys the long dead art of conversation. Just hit record.

160   ABOVE: A former hotel room on the top floor above Martini Beach where I encountered the ghostly bartender. OPPOSITE: The old staircase leading up to Julia's rooms .

TIME MEANS NOTHING to a ghost. A ghost carries with him everything he owns. Time is part of the physical world, and a ghost exists somewhere outside of time. At least that is my theory.

No one knows for sure just what a ghost is. I think ghosts are fields of energy with a consciousness. Our personality and memories seem to be stored in this energy, and they travel with us once the body has finished its run. Whether we cross over and return to Earth in spirit form or choose to stay Earthbound as a ghost, we are who we are. Souls stay intact, persona and all.

I do not go to the beach searching for ghosts. I go to relax and enjoy the surf, sand and ocean air. Daytime on the beach in Cape May is a psychic traffic jam. Even if I wanted to look for a ghost I would not be able to find one in all the chaotic energy that the living give off. Should I be walking on the beach at night when the surf is the only sound and the moon and stars are the light, I can get my psychic bearings and if I happen upon a ghost or vice versa, I will be ready to communicate.

The ghosts like it when people are not around to hoard their space. Some notice us and others ignore us. Some are out for a stroll, while others remain tortured and stuck to the places where they drowned or met some other untimely death by the sea. The beaches in Cape May are always crowded, no matter if that crowd is alive — or dead.

20TH CENTURY HAUNTS

The Modern Era of Ghosts

THE 20TH CENTURY brought some major changes to Cape May. Automobiles slowly replaced the trains and the steamships as a way into town. New construction sprang up in the eastern section of Cape May. A new harbor was dug and old marshland filled in for development. Like the rest of the country, Cape May County would also endure two World Wars. Many of the buildings in Cape May were used by the military as lodging for troops or hospitals for the wounded during the wars. Quite a few wartime ghosts still haunt the beaches and buildings in town. The wars never ended for some of these poor souls.

Another big 20th Century event in Cape May was the weather. Great storms like the Hurricane of 1944 and the Nor'easter of 1962 wreaked havoc on the town. The Borough of South Cape May was literally dissolved in 1944. It had been taking a beating from the pounding surf since the early 1900s. By the time the bunker was built it was (and still is) the only building left standing, in that old summer community to the west of Cape May City. Some of the South Cape May houses were saved and moved into town. The people who died in South Cape May *could* still be haunting these surviving homes. Those ghosts who may have found themselves without a home after South Cape May washed away probably picked up and floated elsewhere — luckily for us.

The 20th century certainly added its share of ghosts to Cape May, and I have encountered many of them on the beaches. Some ghosts are still swimming in the surf, while others play or rest on the beach. Some of the lost souls wander aimlessly, trying to figure out what has become of them. Many ghosts on the beaches seem to be of a transient nature. Some come to the shore for the same reasons that the living do. Others are stuck in past life traumas. Psychically watching ghosts walking on the beach is about as interesting for me as watching paint dry. However, once these disembodied souls decide to call it a day and head inland, the real fun begins. The sun goes down, the ghosts get going, and the houses get haunted.

OPPOSITE: Boats anchored in Cape May's man-made harbor, created in the early 20th century.

Most of these ghosts, and there are many on Cape May's long, flat beaches, will cross over to Heaven eventually. When they are good and ready. They may have lived, worked or stayed in Cape May prior to death, but now call Cape May their home. Death tends to be a relocation service for the soul.

Ghosts are the extension of their living personalities. They still think, feel and remember who they were. They still want some form of security and shelter. If you found yourself lost and alone on a beach at night, wouldn't you try to find shelter? Wouldn't the nearest lights draw you in like a moth to a flame? Ghosts try to reestablish old life patterns quickly after death. They will find a new home.

In life, we get comfortable living in the same house. Human beings are creatures of habit and many are not fond of change. Ghosts are also creatures of habit, but when one's life ends abruptly and he or she is nowhere near home or familiar surroundings, that soul eventually has to give in to the realization that one can never go home again. At some point, these souls learn to adapt to their new world. Heaven is probably always an option, but for some reason many earthbound souls want to stay right where they are.

While it is fanciful to think that every dark corner, attic, cellar and crawlspace in Cape May is harboring ghosts, the fact is, ghosts are more likely to be standing next to you — reading this book. People generally do not want to live under piers or in damp crawl spaces. I am sure most ghosts prefer nice surroundings. There are of course exceptions to everything in the ghost world.

In Cape May, if you do encounter a ghost on the beach, chances are you may also encounter that same ghost, at another time, haunting a house or building in town. Our ghosts get around. They may even follow you if you're nice.

LEFT: Craig at the cove chatting with a (living) seagull.
OPPOSITE: The haunted World War II Bunker at the cove.

WORLD WAR II has left some interesting pockets of paranormal activity in Cape May, and the old bunker is the centerpiece of this activity. Here is one spot where ghosts are hiding within and underneath a building (see right,) and they are enjoying every minute of it.

The huge concrete bunker (right) is home to various ghosts and a few of them seem to be in uniform, leading me to believe they were left over from the war. At one point this part of the beach was about 900 feet back, and the bunker was actually buried in the sand dunes until erosion made it prime beachfront property. Nothing in Cape May stays buried for long.

I have not been able to verify that anyone died in the bunker during the war, but for some reason these ghostly men in uniform still guard the place. They are very aware of passers by and have been known to call out the names of the living, who may wander into their space. Some ghosts are name callers. Why they call out to the living by name and never follow up with anything else is a mystery. Maybe they do it just to bother us. This group is unique in that they know they are dead. They are haunting the bunker in a true sense, and they seem to enjoy the reaction they get from those sensitive enough to "hear" them. This is one spot in Cape May where I have experienced a *psychic storm* of thoughts. It is as if these ghosts knew how to jam my psychic wavelengths. Probably a bunch of dead ex-radio operators from the army.

FARTHER SOUTH, another lone and haunted sentinel, also left over from World War II, harbors its own share of ghosts. Fire Control Tower #23 (pictured left) has stood, isolated and alone since the final days of World War II.

In 2009, the Mid-Atlantic Center for the Arts will be reopening the old fire control tower and everyone will finally be able to climb the old stairs again — and experience the gunning ghosts from another era. I have sensed several ghosts coming and going to this tower, but the thought of scaling a ladder on the outside of the tower never really appealed to me. Now that MAC has restored the interior of the old tower, we will be able to join the ghosts and check out the great view. I will be investigating this tower very shortly and reporting my findings on my website craigmcmanus. com and in future writings. In the meantime, you can do a little ghost hunting yourself.

Horror movies have forever poisoned our imaginations when it comes to hauntings. Remove the Hollywood factor of dead Irish servants rattling chains throughout a house. I know for a fact my deceased relatives would *never* be caught rattling chains. Beer mugs and pinochle decks maybe, but never chains.

Hollywood has created stereotypical images of ghosts and hauntings. Even the word *haunt* is a pejorative — a bum rap for ghosts. Most of the time, ghosts are not out to haunt anyone, with the exception of when the living get on their nerves.

The Hotel Macomber

FINDING A ROOM with a view in Cape May during the summer season is a lot more difficult than finding a room with a *boo* during the dead of winter. When the ghosts are not out on the town, they are usually back in whatever they call *home* at the moment—several call the Hotel Macomber home.

I have a lot of fond memories of staying at the Macomber. Besides being a paranormal hot spot, it's one of the best deals in town for lodging. There are about five different ghosts inhabiting the building at any given time.

The basement has a leftover serviceman the tenants call "the growler" for his penchant for making growling noises. I think he is leftover from the days when the basement of The Macomber was used as a drunk tank during World War II. The drunk servicemen would be locked up for the night in a holding room in the front of the hotel, under the porch. I have sensed several ghosts in uniform at the hotel over the years. Since the military used this facility for a few years during WWII, this could be *residual energy.*

The ghost who haunts Room 10, Irene Wright, also calls on The Sea Villa and The Parris Inn. In life, it is thought that she stayed at all three places. She loved Cape May, and we know she stayed at The Hotel Macomber for many years. Ghosts can also be attached to a place they love and Cape May and Miss Wright have an eternal love affair going strong.

The Hotel Macomber's story is featured in *The Ghosts of Cape May Book 1*. It is even more fun to read the story while staying there. Keep the lights lit.

LEFT: Room 10 at The Macomber—Miss Wright's favorite.
OPPOSITE: The Hotel Macomber on Beach and Howard.

The Inn of Cape May

ATHE...
Restaurant

175

THE INN OF CAPE MAY was built in two parts at the turn of the nineteenth century by the Church brothers. It was constructed on the site of cottages, lost in the Great Fire of 1878, on Ocean Street and Beach Avenue. Staying at the Inn of Cape May is like stepping back in time. As a matter of fact, that's exactly what may happen to you — the ghosts here have a way of making you forget the present.

The Inn is haunted by a woman who is seen wearing a blue dress and may be one of the original servants of the hotel. She has also been caught several times on film, something that rarely happens with ghosts. I am not talking about "orbs." I mean the lady in blue herself appears in pictures. Check out my website channelcraig.com and take a look for yourself.

The fifth floor seems to be the most haunted here. I spent one late night during my Elderhostel course camped out on the fifth floor with my recording equipment. After hearing people talking in one of the rooms nearby and the lights coming on under their door, I decided not to invade anyone's privacy and snuck back down stairs with my equipment. The next morning, when I asked the front desk who was on the fifth floor, the response was, "No one is staying up there this week." Next time I'll knock.

When you stay at The Inn of Cape May, you might run into two noisy children playing ball in the long corridors at night. Don't be concerned by the fact that they're dead. They're both really nice kids. Stuff like this happens all the time in Cape May. Just another day at the beach and this is a great place to stay.

LEFT: One of the enchanted rooms. OPPOSITE: Something on the stairs.

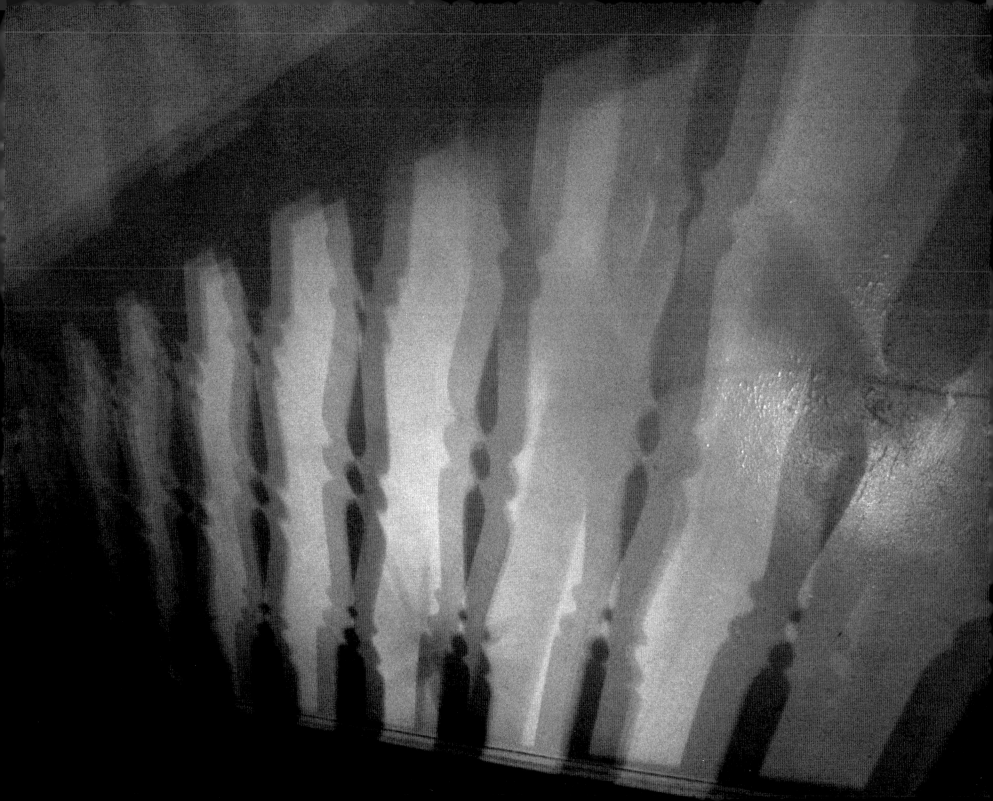

The Peter Shields Inn

PETER SHIELDS built his grand and stately mansion overlooking the ocean in the newly developed east end of Cape May in the early 20th century. The great house, with its towering white columns is now one of Cape May's classier inns.

The ghost here is not a former servant or guest. It is the ghost of Peter's son, Earle Shields, who died from a hunting accident at the young age of 15.

Earle Shields had gone against his father's wishes hunting for marsh hens with friends in the back bays. As he stepped from the smaller dingy into the larger boat they were using, the shotgun he used as a crutch to climb up to the larger boat accidently fired and shot young Shields in the face. He lingered for many hours with every doctor in Cape May on hand to try to save him. They failed and he passed away later that evening.

It is hard to kill a young and energetic spirit. No matter how old the person is, if the spirit strives to live, then live it shall whether or not there is a body to go along for the ride.

Earle is still young at heart and stays in his old house hoping to be reunited with his family someday. It has been over one hundred years since they left him. A wandering ghost, on the eastern shores of Cape May. Someday perhaps, young Mr. Shields will go home.

179

IHAVE LONG SUSPECTED that ghosts are communal beings. I have recorded several ghosts talking with each other, and I have sensed groups of ghosts interacting. There is no reason to believe that ghosts do not socialize. We are all creatures of habit and most of us subscribe to the human trait of *herd mentality*. Ghosts are in a herd of their own, especially in Cape May.

Several groups of haunted houses exist in Cape May. By "groups" I mean houses that are either contiguous or in close proximity. In some cases, like with the two houses on this spread and the previous spread, the properties share a common link with one original owner. If the ghosts originated with this original owner or from a time when the pieces of land were all one property, the hauntings in neighboring houses may be related. The ghosts may also be related to each other as well.

ABOVE: The Purple House and the Yellow House in Eldredge and Broadway. OPPOSITE: The Yellow House

The houses on this page sit on land that was originally part of the Thomas Eldredge Jr. portion of the vast Judith Eldredge estate. In fact, the purple house (left) is yet another Eldredge house built in the 1870s. (I know this is not 20th century house, but the ghost is.)

Barbara Morgan's "yellow house" around the corner was built in the early 20th century on the remaining piece of undeveloped land that was also part of the Thomas Eldredge, Jr. homestead. All three houses are haunted. The purple house is next door to the Eldredge House on Broadway in West Cape May. The yellow house is behind the Thomas Eldredge House. You still with me?

The Thomas Eldredge, Jr. House and the yellow house are covered at length in *The Ghosts of Cape May, Book 3*. The purple house will be in *Book 4*, due out in June of 2010.

I had a most unique experience, a first for my ghost hunting in Cape May, at the purple house. Both Todd Land who owns the Eldredge House and Barbara Morgan who owns the yellow house had been wanting me to check out their neighbor Nick's purple house. Todd spoke to Nick and got permission to bring me into the house for a *mini-investigation*.

It was a balmy 60 degree Sunday in February as we entered the house and found the temperature to be a crisp *42 degrees*. I walked through the house from top to bottom, sensing a man on the third floor. When I returned to the living room on the first floor I stood silently, tape running, and asked a few questions. As I started to ask the ghost questions, doors started to slam upstairs. One of the best door slams I have ever recorded! As I sent out psychic probes, a set of heavy footsteps stormed down the stairs and toward the front door! After that, the house went dead *silent*.

I knew what happened; the damn ghost walked right out on me! I have been insulted on tape, pushed and poked, but never before did I have a ghost walk out on me. Talk about rude. Dying did nothing to mellow this ghost.

I'll be back.

Flanegan's Art and Framing Shop

ONE OF THE MOST HAUNTED spots in Cape May is Diane and Rich Flanegan's Art and Framing shop in West Cape May. By *most haunted* I don't mean ghosts are flying in and out of the windows. It means the paranormal energy here is palpable. For whatever reason the ghosts are more accessible here, especially in one former bathroom.

Upstairs, there is an old side porch bathroom packing quite a paranormal punch. You won't see dead Irish maids floating through the room with trays of ghostly scones. Instead you might sense something heavy or thick in the air (no bathroom jokes please.) This room is quite charged. Within the last fifty years, we think that a young boy drowned in a large iron tub that was once in this room. My EVPs have yielded what sounds like a boy struggling to get out of water, yelling "Let me up!" The tub is now gone, and all that remains of the old bathroom is an ancient steam radiator.

Old timers in West Cape May remember something happening, but nothing specific. The room is active enough that one day it even sent the Flanagan's plumber running out the front door of the house! A mystery yet to be solved.

The ghost of Annie Hand Bishop, one of the early owners of the house, also resides here. Her energy is very positive, like that of a kind grandmother. Maybe she *is* a mother figure for the young ghost. If she knows who the child is, she is not talking. Was it one of her family members? Does she stay to watch over him? Something is keeping both Annie and the boy tethered to this house. Annie and her adult son ran a general store next to the house in the early 20th century. Could they still be working? Why do they still haunt their old haunt?

I suggest a visit to Flanagan's Art studio, it is a great place to watch both artists (and ghosts) at work.

ABOVE: The old iron radiator still hissing away in the haunted bathroom at Flanegan's Art and Framing pictured opposite.

The Albert Stevens Inn

THE DOCTOR *is in.* At least his ghost is. Dr. Albert Gateton Stevens was a well-known and much loved local Doc who worked in the field of homeopathy. He obviously also discovered a cure for death, as his ghost, and that of his daughter Vesta, still linger around their old homestead on Myrtle Avenue in West Cape May.

Not much has changed here since the house was built around 1900, with the exception that it is now one of Cape May's top Bed & Breakfasts run with great care by Jim & Lenanne Labrusciano. The house, like many buildings in Cape May, has been beautifully restored and well preserved. This continuity could be another reason why Cape May is so haunted. Things have not changed much and the ghosts still feel like they had never (physically) left.

I have often wondered if a man of science or medicine would deliberately stay put as a ghost to explore a side of nature he had not experienced in life. If Dr. Stevens was such an accomplished man of medicine in his day and in his community, is it possible that the only thing keeping him stuck on the Earth Plane is pure curiosity?

The fact that he was a doctor also brings up the question, do ghosts need medical attention in the afterlife? We really don't know what a ghost is.

The theory is that a ghost is a field of energy with conscious thought and personality. We have people who are energy healers here on the Earth Plane, once a person dies and becomes pure energy, could

LEFT: A (ghost) doctor in the house — Dr. Albert G. Stevens.
(Courtesy of Jim & Lenanne Labrusciano)

they too become an energy healer to others in the Ghost Realm?

My psychic read on Dr. Stevens has been that he is either a ghost or a spirit come back from Heaven to help those stuck here as ghosts. He radiates intelligence, and his presence is very strong. The ghost of his daughter Vesta, who died much more recently, has a soft, sweet energy about her and seems to stay in the background. The Doc is not a mean man, just intense. His portrait to the left says it all! Is this man of medical science still practicing in the afterlife? I wonder if he takes Boo Cross and Boo Shield?

ABOVE: A vintage photograph of the old Stevens home.
(Courtesy of Jim & Lenanne Labrusciano)

The Wilbraham Mansion

JOHN WILBRAHAM IS DEAD. But then again, so is everyone else who haunts Cape May. A Philadelphia iron magnate, Wilbraham decided to expand his little Cape May farmhouse to create a majestic this mansion around 1900.

He lived in the house with his wife, Ann, whom he had married after his brother, Ann's first husband, died. It is Ann Wilbraham and two children who reside here, almost one hundred years after their deaths. Why she haunts is a mystery, she communicates very little on the psychic level.

My first experience with the ghosts here was when I stayed in the third floor suite that at one time was the servants' quarters. I fell asleep late at night only to be awakened by noises in the room. When I lit the light I saw nothing unusual, with the exception that a small rocking chair had been moved closer to the bed. Now I suppose I could have gotten up in my sleep and done it, but I have not been known to sleepwalk. Was something coming near the bedside to make contact?

Ghosts often try to talk with us in our dreams. If you have ever been away from home and had strange dreams of talking to people you did not recognize, you may have been communicating with a ghost. There have been several times when I have been in a haunted house where I could not make contact with the ghosts, only to have the ghosts contact me later in my dreams.

When we dream, there is a suspension of disbelief. The ghosts appear to us as living, breathing people, so we typically engage them in conversation. It is only upon waking that we realize we have been talking to the dead. Regrettably, we rarely remember all of our dreams, and most of our nocturnal ghost encounters vanish from our minds as quickly as the ghosts themselves.

Samuel R. Ludlam House

S PENDING THE NIGHT in a haunted house is always an adventure, spending a week in a haunted house—especially when that house is Ludlam House in Cape May—is the trip of a lifetime! Cape May has hundreds of great haunts all over town, but this mansion on the outskirts of the main section of the city is hustling and bustling with paranormal energy.

Samuel R. Ludlam is well known in the annals of Cape May history. His Ocean House Hotel, built before the Civil War, was the place where the Great Fire of 1878 began. Ludlam was last seen boarding a train for his winter home in Dennisville shortly before the blaze began. He had recently heavily insured the structure. The fire destroyed more than 30 acres of prime Cape May resort property. Most of the hotels

THE OCEAN HOUSE.
PROPRIETOR, SAMUEL R. LUDLAM, CAPE MAY CITY, N.J.

were destroyed including Congress Hall and the Columbia Hotel. Ludlam was brought to trial, but released on a lack of evidence. Ironically, the fire stopped at just the corner where Ludlam's summer home stood, directly across the street from Dr. Ware's Drugstore. It is said the flames licked the sides of the house, but it did not catch fire.

After the ordeal, Ludlam divorced his wife and moved back to Dennisville. The house was sold and enlarged by the next owner. In the early 1900s "Ludlam House" as I call it, was moved *on logs pulled by mules* from the corner of Columbia and Ocean to the corner of Jefferson and Kearney. In those days wood was much more expensive than labor, and this house was worth moving.

I cannot say for sure which of the previous owners, family members or servants are haunting this great old mansion, but I can say they are haunting it well! I love this house. I love the energy and the fact that it has such a wonderfully dicey history just makes me like it even more.

A young girl named Sophie or Sophia is one of the resident ghosts here. A picture purchased by the current owner, Cathy Force, looks very much like the image I see of the little girl when she is near. There are also several ghostly servants "living" in the quarters under the house. The fact that they are here may mean they worked for the owners after Ludlam, who had the house raised and improved in 1907. The paneled chapel room in the front tower, with its stained glass windows seems to be a favorite of both the living and the dead. I spent the week sleeping in this otherworldly room, and I can tell you phantom footsteps were the least of my ghostly experience! You can read the whole story in *The Ghosts of Cape May Book 3*.

190

ABOVE: Postcard of Ludlam's Ocean House Hotel (Author's Collection) OPPOSITE: The fabulous Samuel R. Ludlam House on Jefferson and Kearney. NEXT SPREAD: The chapel Room and the painted walls going up the great staircase.

839

21ST CENTURY HAUNTS

A Work in Progress

ONE THING a ghost hunter should always do is respect the privacy of the living. If I find that a ghost is extremely contemporary, I will omit the names or even the entire report of the investigation. While it is enjoyable to read about ghosts from fifty or one hundred years ago, having someone stumble upon a report of their recently deceased loved one haunting somewhere would *not* be very professional on my part.

I have encountered ghosts of people in Cape May who have died within the last few years. They are stuck for the same reasons as all of the other ghosts in town. Sometimes family members know they are still around, while other times those same family members think that their loved ones have gone on to Heaven. Some of us just take longer to get the trip made than others. I cannot even say for sure where Heaven is or if it allows souls that have passed to come back to Earth and spend more time in their old haunts.

Therefore, while there are wonderful stories of newly made ghosts of the 20th and early 21st centuries in Cape May, you will have to wait a few more years before you will see those reports from this writer. Out of respect to living family members, these cases must remain closed.

Of course there are many more ghosts to come to our quaint little seaside resort. Each new year brings a herd of new souls saying goodbye to the physical world and crossing over. As history does repeat itself, many of these souls will be taking a detour back to Cape May.

At what point will America's oldest seaside resort have an overcrowding problem with ghosts? At the rate things are going, inn keepers and B & B owners will have to start charging for ghostly guests! Will a time come when the dead outnumber the living in Cape May?

If you or I decide to come back and haunt the peninsula, what will we see? Will the town look exactly as it does now or will it look like it does when we die? Unfortunately, the only way we will know what happens when we die is by experiencing it first hand. Everything else is only conjecture. I don't know about you, but I have a lot more work to do on this Earth Plane before I plan to check out.

There is some reason, only known to the dead, why Cape May is so haunted. They roam the streets at night, lurk in the dark recesses of old buildings and alleyways and move freely in and around the living, rarely being noticed. Why are they here? Do they know our names? Do they know who is next to join them? Are you on the list?

OPPOSITE: A stormy day in old Cape May makes the new ghosts come out and play.

4HUNDRED YEARS ago there were probably ghosts in Cape May and four hundred years from now people will still be writing about them. No one really knows what ghosts are or why they exist. All we have is theories and an unquenchable thirst for the unknown. Someday we may know the truth. Perhaps then we will know why many of the dead people in the photograph to the right (it was taken in 1886, that's why they're all dead) are still haunting the resort they loved during the time they lived. What special hold does Cape May have over all of us who love to come here so much?

ONLY TIME will tell what will become of America's oldest seaside resort and her ghosts. Cape May's cool beaches and quaint Victorian architecture, fabulous hotels, charming Bed and Breakfasts, wonderful restaurants and shops will continue to draw in crowds of future generations of beach lovers. Cape May's ghosts will also continue to attract those paranormal enthusiasts who want to know more about things that go bump in the surf. Maybe we all just keep coming back to old Cape May, in this life and in the next, some of us even getting a little extra time in as ghosts.

ON HENRY HUDSON'S final voyage to America in 1610, searching one more time for the famed Northwest Passage, he and his crew encountered harsh weather conditions in the Hudson Bay region and wintered on land until June of 1611. Hudson wanted to continue the exploration, but his crew refused and mutinied, setting Hudson and some loyal crew mates adrift in a small boat in the Hudson Bay. No one knows what happened to Henry Hudson afterward. It is presumed he died. I am sure Henry Hudson, should he be haunting the shores of the Hudson Bay, would much rather be haunting the shores of warm Cape May. See Henry, you should have spent more than a night in town. Now it's time to start hitchhiking south.

History has left us with no visual record of Henry Hudson. All we have is accounts of his voyages and life. Ghosts also leave no visual record and, like Hudson, their stories will continue to be told to generations to come. The ghosts of Cape May will live on through these stories, and their lives and their part in the history of Cape May will be preserved forever—right along with them. America's oldest and most haunted seaside resort lives on. I hope you have enjoyed this compendium of haunts. This was a much bigger project than I had imagined. I now realize I am incapable of "writing snippets and short passages" for a work that should be more pictures than words—I am much too big a windbag for that. My coffee table book runneth over. What you have here is less coffee table and more *Kaffeeklatsch*. I hope you have enjoyed the long chat.

Until next time, keep enjoying all the wonderful things that beautiful Cape May has to offer—and don't forget to leave the light lit—some of those things may be reading over your shoulder. C. M.

OPPOSITE: Beach scene taken from the old Iron Pier in the late 1880s that originally appeared in an 1895 travel guide. Congress Hall is on the extreme right and The Light of Asia or "old jumbo" the elephant on the left in what was once South Cape May. (Author's collection)

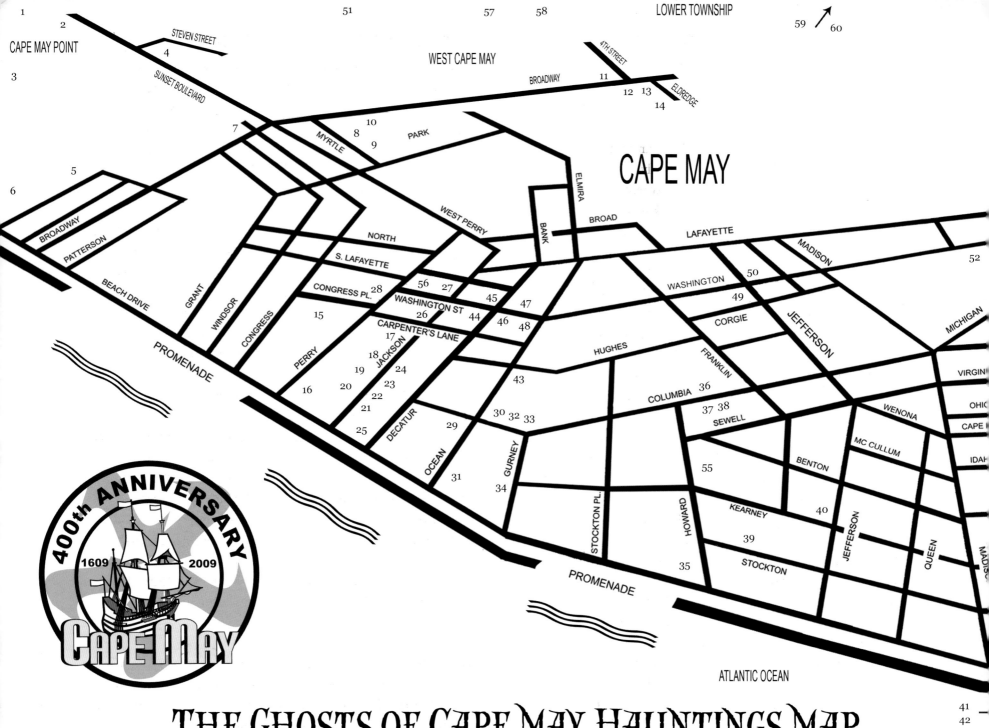

THE GHOSTS OF CAPE MAY HAUNTINGS MAP

Cape May's 400th Anniversary Logo designed by Kathy DeLuccia

NAME OF HAUNT	ACCESSIBILITY
1. Sunset Beach	Open to the public
2. Fire Control Tower #23	Open to the public (MAC)
3. The Lighthouse	Open to the public (MAC)
4. The Old Reeves Homestead	No - Private Residence
5. Site of the Mount Vernon	Yes - Bird Sanctuary
6. The World War II Bunker	Exterior Only
7. The Whilldin-Miller House	Yes - Restaurant
8. The Albert Stevens Inn	Yes - Bed & Breakfast
9. The Wilbraham Mansion	Yes - Bed & Breakfast
10. Highland House	Yes - Guest House
11. Flanagan's Art & Framing	Yes - Retail Shop
12 Thomas Eldredge House	Yes - Guest House
13. The Purple House	Yes - Summer Rental
14. The Yellow House	No - Private Residence
15. Congress Hall Hotel	Yes - Historic Hotel
16. The Sea Villa	Yes - Guest Rooms
17. The Merry Widow	Yes - Guest Suites
18. The Saltwood House	Yes - Bed & Breakfast
19. Windward House	Yes - Bed & Breakfast
20. Inn at 22 Jackson	Yes - Part of the Virginia Hotel
21. The John McConnell House	No - Private Residence
22. Poor Richards Inn	Yes - Bed & Breakfast
23. The Carroll Villa	Yes - Historic Hotel
24. The Virginia Hotel	Yes - Historic Hotel
25. Cabanas/Martini Beach	Yes - Restaurants & Bars
26. The Capital Hotel Building	Yes - Now Fralinger's Taffy
27. Former candle shop	Yes - Still a retail store
28. The Parris Inn	No - Now Private
29. Columbia House	Yes - Guest Suites
30. The House of Royals	Yes - Bed & Breakfast
31. The Inn of Cape May	Yes - Historic Hotel
32. The John F. Craig House	Yes - Bed & Breakfast
33. The Mason Cottage	Yes - Bed & Breakfast

NAME OF HAUNT	ACCESSIBILITY
34. The Belvidere Cottage	Yes - Summer Rental
35. The Hotel Macomber	Yes - Historic Hotel
36. The Linda Lee	Yes - Bed & Breakfast
37. The Bacchus Cottage	Yes - Bed & Breakfast
38. The Jacob leaming House	No - Private Residence
39. The Sea Holly Inn	No - Private Residence
40. Samuel R. Ludlam House	Yes - Summer Rental
41. Angel of the Sea	Yes - Bed & Breakfast
42. Peter Shields Inn	Yes - Bed & Breakfast/Restaurant
43. The Fairthorne Cottage	Yes - Bed & Breakfast
44. The Ugly Mug	Yes - Bar and Restaurant
45. Lace Silhouettes/Cotton Co.	Yes - Retail Stores
46. Atlantic Books	Yes - Book Store
47. CapeMay.com	No - Offices
48. Winterwood & Ticket Booth	Yes - Gift Shop
49. The Southern Mansion	Yes - Bed & Breakfast
50. The Washington Inn	Yes - Restaurant
51. Site of the Town Bank Colony	Yes - Bay
52. The Emlen Physick Estate	Yes - Tours by MAC/Gift Shop
53. Hadrava House	No - Private Residence
54. The John Hand House	Yes - Summer Rental
55. The Chalfonte Hotel	Yes - Historic Hotel
56. The Seahorse	No - Private Residence
57. Isaac Smith, Jr. House	No - Private Residence
58. David Cresse House	No - Private Residence
59. Historic Cold Spring Village	Yes - Outdoor Museum
60. Cold Spring Church	Yes - Church and graveyard

Please respect private property. The owners of some of these haunts live on the premises. Kindly respect their privacy and please do not trespass on their private property. There are plenty of other haunts that are open to the public on this map that you can explore. Happy Haunting!